ICT in @ction

Kate Norman
and Stuart Ball

ages 5–7

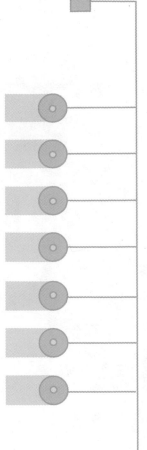

Authors
Stuart Ball and Kate Norman

Editor
David Sandford

Assistant Editor
Christine Harvey

Series designer and cover artwork
Joy Monkhouse

Designer
Mark Udall

CD programming
Symbiosis

Clip Art
© Corel

MADE WITH
macromedia®

acknowledgements

The publishers would like to thank the Parents Information Network for permission to reproduce their Health and Safety information on pages 9 and 10. Copyright © Parents Information Network (PIN) 2000. All rights reserved.

Every effort has been made to trace copyright holders and the publishers apologise for any omissions.

In production, every effort has been made to ensure that websites and addresses referred to in this book are correct and educationally sound. They are believed to be current at the time of publication. The publishers cannot be held responsible for subsequent changes in the address of a website, nor for the content of the sites mentioned. Referral to a website is not an endorsement by the publisher of that site.

Text © 2002 Stuart Ball and Kate Norman
© 2002 Scholastic Ltd

Designed using Adobe Pagemaker

Published by Scholastic Ltd,
Villiers House,
Clarendon Avenue,
Leamington Spa,
Warwickshire CV32 5PR

Printed by Bell & Bain Ltd, Glasgow

2 3 4 5 6 7 8 9 0   2 3 4 5 6 7 8 9 0 1

British Library Cataloguing-in-Publication Data. A catalogue record for this book is available from the British Library.

ISBN 0-439-01982-6

Visit our website at www.scholastic.co.uk

Contents

Introduction

ICT in the primary school

Since September 2000, information technology has been referred to as information communication technology. The addition of the letter 'C' has signalled a change in emphasis in the way we use IT in the classroom: the computer is now a tool for pupils to communicate their thoughts and ideas. But the ICT curriculum also aims to highlight how the computer can be used to enhance teaching and learning across the whole curriculum, so the letter 'C' could also represent Curriculum or Content as well as Communication.

So how, as teachers, do we ensure that we develop children's IT skills and make ICT an integral part of learning? This is an issue that is made more difficult when many teachers feel that pupils know more about computers than they do, and when the vast array of software available seems to present an impossible range of skills that need to be acquired to ensure effective delivery of ICT in the classroom. These issues need not prove insurmountable, though, and can quite easily be overcome with a more focused strategy for using IT in the curriculum. This book has an approach to ICT based on the following ideas:

❑ using software that is familiar to teachers, children and parents
❑ delivering the curriculum through a core of common applications
❑ introducing ideas that can be used, adapted and extended
❑ providing ready-made files to use in the classroom
❑ showing how to create your own versions of these activities to use in the classroom.

A software toolbox

Many classrooms will already have a 'toolbox' of props, stationery and books that can be used and adapted to deliver the various demands of the curriculum – why not use computer software in the same way? A few common software packages, ones that often come pre-installed on computers, can be used in many different ways and can provide differentiated learning opportunities, delivering assessment criteria across the curriculum.

What should a basic software toolbox contain? In the primary classroom you will need:

❑ a word processor
❑ a desktop publishing package
❑ a spreadsheet package
❑ a database package
❑ a presentation package
❑ a graphics package
❑ access to the Internet and e-mail.

These simple applications are essentially all that you need, and can be used in the classroom to make resources and activities that children can use to develop their ICT skills.

Rather than letting children use 'educational' versions of such types of software, there are many benefits to be gained if the software used by teacher and pupil are the same. Skills that need to be taught to the children can be 'tried and tested' by the teacher; and many children will have similar software on their home PCs, thus making practice of these skills at home possible and preparing children for using software in real-life contexts. While this software may not always be

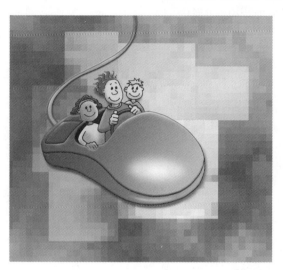

seen as the best tool for the job, or even seen as 'educational' software in the accepted sense of the phrase, it does allow teachers to utilise their acquired skills – especially those from NOF – to maximum effect. This is what the ideas in this book aim to demonstrate: that with a little knowledge, common software can be put to educational use without the need to invest in expensive dedicated programs. The ideas provided are backed up by relevant resources on the CD that accompanies this book. The files on the CD aim to show how to use skills learned in *Microsoft Office* and *Windows* to develop relevant activities for the classroom.

What do they do?

As a software 'toolbox', the basic *Office* applications provide teachers, and ultimately children, the tools they need to use ICT to communicate their thoughts and ideas across the whole curriculum.

Word processors

A word processor can be used to produce reports, stories or poems, but this can be a lengthy process as children are rarely speedy typists and simply copying up a piece of written work is perhaps the ICT equivalent of colouring in!

Word processors are best used to produce short, direct statements through the use of wordbanks and copying and pasting, or as a means by which children can save their 'work in progress' after short sessions at the screen, allowing them to go back to their work and add to or redraft it later. A word processor is also a useful tool when children are collecting information from reference materials and copying and pasting information from a CD-ROM or a website. This information can then be re-read, and the relevant information can be selected and edited using a word processor so it can be incorporated into their work.

Introduction

To an extent word processors, and more specifically desktop publishing (DTP) programs, are ideal to allow work to be presented in a different way, such as a newspaper report, a collaborative report, or an historic-looking document through the use of different fonts and layout. When using a word processor, children can work as a group – each contributing their thoughts and ideas. This approach can be made more effective if an adult is available to type the comments made.

A word processor can also be a great leveller and motivator, providing children who may have difficulties writing with an outlet to express their ideas more easily, helping them with spelling and presentation and allowing them to concentrate on the content of their work.

Spreadsheets and graphing programs

Spreadsheets are highly versatile programs. They can be used to analyse data and represent it in graphical form, to model real-life situations or to keep records and plot progress. Spreadsheets have the functionality to allow automatic calculations, such as totals and averages, making them very powerful tools for use in the classroom and allowing teachers and pupils to create and explore mathematical models with ease.

A graphing program does much the same job as a spreadsheet, but perhaps more simply: children can enter their results into a table and, depending on the program, choose to display the results as a graph of their choice. By producing a simple bar graph, children instantly have a visual representation of the data collected from their investigations: this allows younger children to make comparisons between values and provides a means by which they can begin to analyse data, with the opportunity to draw conclusions. This is important, as young children often do not have the coordination skills to draw effective graphs, and using the computer enables them to experience working with graphs in science, history and numeracy.

Database programs

A database can be thought of as something that stores a wide range of information that can be searched, sorted and analysed. This could be anything from the children's favourite snacks to an encyclopaedia on a CD-ROM, or even the Internet. Children can collect information about themselves, or any other topic such as minibeasts or books, which can be entered into a database program. They can then use the database to find out the answers to questions such as 'How many children have blue eyes?' Creating a database from scratch can be a lengthy process, but using prepared templates or databases downloaded from the Internet can make their use easier and allow children to focus on questioning the database rather than the intricacies of creating the structure and filling it with information.

Presentation software

Microsoft PowerPoint can be a powerful tool in the classroom to share familiar nursery rhymes with the children, as shown in Chapter 9.

Using an application such as *Microsoft PowerPoint* allows teachers to make truly interactive multimedia displays, creating animated lessons, worksheets and books that can bring a story or subject to life. Children can also create their own presentations or interactive quizzes, using multimedia elements such as pictures, text, sound, and video to present their ideas and thoughts about different subject areas to the rest of the class.

The *PowerPoint* activities in Chapter 9, 'Animated books' show how ICT can bring simple stories and nursery rhymes to life as multimedia books. These can greatly enhance children's enjoyment of stories, and can be used with whole classes, small groups of children or individuals. At Key Stage 1, children may not be able to create their own presentations, but using *PowerPoint* as a display tool can be an extremely useful and beneficial practice both for shared reading and for children to interact and engage with stories that you have created yourself.

Graphics programs

These include drawing and painting packages and programs that can manipulate images. Graphics packages range from simple painting programs such as *Paint*, to advanced image manipulation software and 3-D modelling packages. They may be used in conjunction with a digital camera or a scanner, a library of images on CD-ROM or images downloaded from the Internet, and they can be used to create not only artwork but plans, diagrams and maps. Some image manipulation programs often offer tools that allow children to create some dramatic images on screen.

Graphics programs can be used for more than simply creating images and manipulating photographs. The basic drawing tools can teach skills such as mouse control, and can allow children to experiment with colour and shape. In conjunction with a scanner, children can also use graphics packages to see their paintings and drawings on the computer screen, and to alter and manipulate these using the software in ways they couldn't on paper.

Access to the Internet and e-mail

These two applications are now making more and more of an impact in the classroom, allowing both children and teachers alike access to a

Introduction

vast resource and enabling them to share information quickly and easily. Children can now communicate with people and access resources from all around the world, and to make full use of this exciting resource children and teachers need to have developed a range of skills that cover the other applications, as well as file handling and desktop management.

How to use this book

Each chapter in this book looks at a different aspect of ICT, and suggests how computer work can be integrated into the course of daily lessons as well as meeting the demands of the ICT curriculum. The curriculum grid on page 16 shows how these skills are linked to the QCA scheme of work for ICT.

The first page of each chapter breaks down the activities and details the resources and vocabulary needed in order to deliver the activity ideas. This page will also tell you what software is required, and where the files that accompany the activities can be found on the CD.

Following this is an introduction and a section looking at the skills that the children will learn from the activities in this chapter, and skills practice activities for the children to work on before tackling the main projects. These may simply be introducing children to a new piece of software or discussing what a computer can be used for, or they may be specific activities looking at skills that will be needed in the rest of the chapter.

The activities are self-contained ideas for lesson plans, backed up by resources on the CD. The lessons are split into four main sections: an introductory session with the whole class that details what is to be done. This may involve a demonstration of the activity at the computer, or a discussion about how computers can be used to fulfil a need. Following this is an activity for children to carry out at the computer in small groups or individually on a rota basis. For those not at the computer, desk-based activities back up the work at the screen. A conclusion that draws the learning together rounds the activity off, and there are ideas for adapting and tailoring the lesson to your current topic work for extension and consolidation.

At the end of each chapter is a workshop section especially for teachers. This will show you, step-by-step, how to create your own versions of the files on the CD, so that you can adapt the ideas for your own needs. All the components needed to create the files are placed on the CD, and the workshop will help you through the process of making the files from scratch using the same software as was used to create the original files on the CD.

Health and safety

There are many health and safety issues associated with use of computers that teachers need to be aware of in the primary classroom. This section outlines some relating directly to the school situation that teachers will need to be aware of, although you should consult your school's policy on computer usage for full guidance.

Posture

Posture is very important and children should be given a few simple guidelines. Make sure they are not constantly leaning their head forward (it is very heavy for the neck to support!), and encourage them to keep the chin tucked in. The back should be supported in an upright position in the chair and the body should face forwards, not twisted sideways. Children sharing a computer should be encouraged to make sure that everyone in the group can see without straining.

Children should take a break from the computer at least every 20 minutes, and do some simple stretching to relieve the muscles they have been using – hands, wrists, neck. It is a good idea to get up and walk around at least once an hour and refresh the eye muscles by looking at distant objects as well as those close up. Children can make these exercises into their own personal 'computer workout' routine.

Suitable hardware

Make sure children know how to adjust a screen for brightness and contrast, and how to position it to avoid glare from lights or windows. They should be looking down at the screen, with the top of the screen roughly at their eye level. There is a slight risk of triggering epileptic seizures from excessive screen flicker – there is wide variation in the 'steadiness' of screen image from one monitor to another, and if an individual child is at risk then consult with the relevant therapist/ doctor when choosing a screen for them to use. All children should have regular eye check-ups.

Show children how to hold the mouse lightly in the widest part of the hand with their fingers resting lightly on the mouse button(s) so that a very small movement is needed to click a button. A small mouse is best for those with small hands. The arm or wrist should be supported on the table or wrist rest and check that they don't extend one or more fingers stiffly as this can lead to muscle strain. If children spend a lot of time using a computer, you should be aware of alternatives to a traditional keyboard and mouse – ergonomic keyboards, voice recognition systems, trackerballs, handwriting recognition pads, finger pads and 'mouse pens'. These should all be available for demonstration at your local computer store. There are

Introduction

various types of wrist rests available that can take the strain off the wrist when typing at a keyboard. Show children how to choose the position of the keyboard that feels most comfortable. Most keyboards can be used at different angles of tilt but the flattest position is best for most wrists.

Functional furniture

When using a computer, a child should be able to sit upright on a chair which gives some back support, having their arms roughly horizontal when using a keyboard. If their feet don't reach the floor, then use a footstool. Ideally, the chair height should be adjustable to suit all the people who will use it.

There should be space on the computer table for the keyboard in front of the monitor, and for a wrist rest in front of the keyboard. Keep the monitor well back from the front edge of the table. There should be enough space on the computer table for a mouse mat, a computer manual, any paperwork, and software disks. A simple document holder can be attached to the monitor to keep paperwork off the work surface.

Reducing risks

Don't be tempted to connect too many extension cables or double socket adapters to your existing electrical sockets – if you are in any doubt at all, call in an electrician to check the safety of your system and always replace damaged plugs or leads. Do uncoil leads but don't leave them trailing on the floor. Explain to children that computer equipment that uses mains electricity must be treated with the same caution as TV sets or electrical equipment in the kitchen.

Check regularly to make sure the computer equipment is sitting in a stable position and hasn't been pushed or tilted too far. Don't use the top of the computer or monitor as a storage shelf as you may block ventilation grills and cause overheating.

This health and safety document is part of the 'Superhighway Safety Pack', the full text of which is held on the National Grid for Learning at: http://safety.ngfl.gov.uk. Written by Jane Mitra © Parents Information Network (PIN) 2000.

How to use the CD

The CD included with this book contains a range of data files and resources that are needed for some of the projects and activities described in this book.

The files can be used in a number of ways, some of which will depend on how your computer is set up and the particular software you have on it. The ways of using the files described here are based on a stand-alone machine in the classroom; to use these files over a network or in a computer suite please consult with your school's network manager.

Before working on any activity, you will need to make a copy of the file and place it on your computer's hard drive (usually C:). From here, depending on how you wish to organise the activity itself, you may need to make further copies of the file for individual children to work on. The CD has a menu program that will allow you to do this automatically, but you can do this for yourself if you wish.

Using the menu program to browse and copy files

When you put the *ICT in @ction* CD into your CD-ROM drive with *Windows* running, the menu should automatically start and present you with a short animation followed by the *ICT in @ction* menu screen. If it doesn't start automatically, click the *Start* menu and choose 'Run', then type D:\scholastic.exe in the window that appears (this assumes that D: is the letter of your CD-ROM drive). Click 'OK' and the menu program will start.

To bypass the menu program, hold down the SHIFT key while the computer is loading the CD; this will allow you to browse the CD as if it were a normal disc using 'My Computer' or *Windows Explorer*, launching files from their position on the CD or copying them as you wish to another location.

Once loaded, the menu will present you with four options:

How to use the CD

This will bring up a brief guide that explains how the CD is organised, and suggests ways of using and storing the files on your classroom computer so that they can be used in lessons. At any point, click 'Back' to return to the main menu screen.

Contents

The 'Contents' option will allow you to browse the files on the CD, and to copy them to your computer for use in lessons. The CD is

Introduction

organised on a chapter-by-chapter basis, with one folder for each chapter of the book, and inside each of these folders is a folder for each activity. All the file and folder names are the same as those used in the book, so you can locate files quickly and easily. There are three columns on the contents screen (as shown on the right).

Use the 'Contents' screen to find the files for the activities you need – they are organised using the same structure and titles as in the book so you can find them easily.

The first column lists the chapters of the book in order. Clicking with the left mouse button on any of the chapters will bring up a list of the activities in this chapter in the second column. Clicking on an activity will list the files associated with the activity in the third column. If you wish, you can preview any of the files listed in the third column by clicking on them with the left mouse button; this will bring up a small thumbnail image in the bottom right-hand corner of the screen showing what the file looks like.

Where the files are copied

At the bottom of the first column is a box telling you where the CD will place files when they are copied to your computer's hard drive. By default, the menu program will create a folder called 'Scholastic ICT In Action' on your hard drive, but you can change this to a more convenient place by clicking the 'Change' button. This will prompt you to enter a different destination folder for the files, although the name of the folder will not change.

Copying files

You can choose whether to copy the files for a whole activity at once, or whether to copy individual files to your computer's hard drive with the 'Copy' buttons underneath the second and third columns. Highlight an activity in the second column and click the 'Copy activity folder' button to copy all the files associated with this activity to your chosen destination folder.

To copy individual files, highlight the activity in the third column (you can select more than one at once: hold down the CTRL key as you click on each additional file in the list to highlight a group of files) and click the 'Copy file' button underneath the third column. This will copy the file or files you have selected to the 'Scholastic ICT in Action' folder on your chosen hard drive.

In each case, the menu program will check to see whether you have the appropriate software installed on your computer, and will warn you if the necessary program is missing (although you will still be able to proceed if you wish). It will also check to ensure that you have enough space on your hard drive to copy the file.

At any point you can click 'Menu' to return to the main menu, or 'Help' for help.

Licence

This will bring up the terms and conditions for using this CD. Using the CD indicates your acceptance of these terms and conditions. This licence is printed inside the book; we recommend that you read this before using any of the files in the classroom. Click 'Menu' to return to the main menu.

Exit

The 'Exit' option will close the menu program and return you to *Windows*, although you can still access the files on the CD through *Windows Explorer* or 'My Computer' as long as the CD is in the drive.

Copying files manually from the CD to your hard drive

All the disk drives on a computer are allocated a letter. The internal hard drive in your computer has the letter C: assigned to it. The floppy disk drive has A:, and the CD-ROM drive usually has the letter D:, but this will depend on the setup of your particular computer. To find the letters assigned to the different drives on your computer, double-click (two quick clicks in succession with the left mouse button) the 'My Computer' icon on the desktop. This will open a window that will look something like this:

Here you will see the hard, floppy and CD-ROM drives with their associated letters and icons. When there is a CD in the drive the icon will show the name of the disk, in this case 'ICT in @ction'.

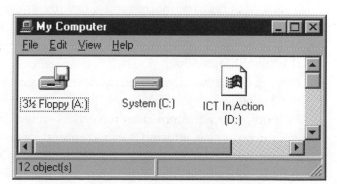

Introduction

Right-click on the CD-ROM drive icon and, from the menu that pops up, choose 'Open' to begin exploring the CD. The activity files are kept in a folder called 'ICT In Action 5-7'; double-click on this icon to open another window that should look like this:

Each chapter in the book has its own folder, inside which are all the relevant activity and resource files for you to complete the projects in that chapter. The file and folder names match those used in the book to make finding the files you want to use as easy as possible.

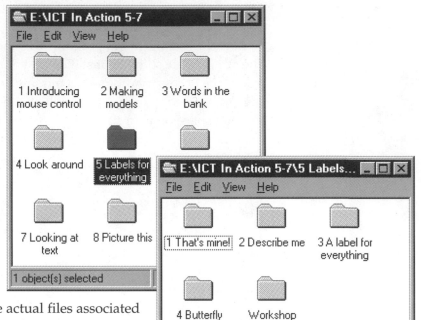

Double-click on a chapter folder; another window will open up showing the files within that folder. Double-click an icon once more to see the actual files associated with this activity. To copy files from the CD to your computer (for example, to the desktop), click on the icon of the file or folder with the left mouse button and, holding the mouse button down, drag the file to where you want it to end up. Let go of the mouse button and the file will be copied. To copy a whole folder with all the files in it, repeat using the whole chapter folder. By having a number of windows open files can be copied from the CD to any location on your hard drive, from where they can be used in lessons, or moved and copied to other locations. The 'File handling and desktop management' chapter on page 17 gives further details on how to move, copy and organise files.

Running a file directly from the CD

To look at files directly from the CD without the need to copy them to your computer, open up the folder containing the file you want to look at as described above. Double-click on the file that you want use; this file will now open directly in the application needed to use it. Bear in mind that if you want to save any changes you make to the file opened from the CD, you will have to save the file to a different location, as you cannot change the files stored on the CD.

This process is affected by a number of factors, though. When a program is installed on a computer, the files it uses are 'associated' with it, so that the computer can recognise a *Microsoft Word* file and make sure that when you double-click the file's icon, *Word* opens automatically and loads the file. If you do not have *Word* installed, though, your computer will not recognise that file and you will be unable to open it. These associations can be changed; see the 'File handling and desktop management' chapter on page 17 for details.

Running a file from the hard drive or desktop

If you have copied files from the CD to your hard drive, either through the menu program or as described above, you can also run the files directly. Make sure the files that you want to use have been copied to your hard drive (as described above), and that you know which folder to find the files in. The process is then exactly the same as for running files from the CD, except that you look in a different folder; this depends on where you have copied the files.

Running a file from within an application

Alternatively, you can choose to run the application first, opening the file from within the program. This makes sure that you use your preferred application for viewing specific types of file. To do this, start the application (for example, *Microsoft Word*) as you would normally – either through the *Start* menu, or from the desktop – then click *File > Open* and select the file you want to open, either from the CD directly or from the folder you have copied the file to.

Troubleshooting

In production of these resources we have checked all the files carefully to ensure that they are fit for their purpose, but should you encounter problems with any of the files on the CD it is likely that there is a simple solution to your problem. In the root directory of the CD there is a file called **Readme.doc**, which details some common problems that you might encounter when using the files and their solutions. Check this file in the first instance, but if the problem persists consult your school's network manager or the suppliers of your system.

If you are running a computer with management software on it, you may get an error message when running the menu program supplied on the CD. If so, it is still possible to use the files on the CD by copying them manually as described above.

Skills practice

It is a useful exercise to practise opening, copying and moving files, as keeping the classroom computer organised is essential. Once you are comfortable with these skills, you could make some prompt cards for children to use outlining the skills. These can be displayed around the computer, giving the children constant reminders of what to do and making them more independent users of the computer.

Curriculum links

Chapter title	QCA unit	National Curriculum for Information Technology (England)	National Curriculum for Information Technology (Wales)	5–14 Guidelines (Scotland)	Programs used	Curriculum subjects used	Yeargroup
Introducing mouse control	All aspects	Knowledge, Skills and Understanding 1a, 2a, 2b, 2d; Breadth of Study 5a, 5b	Communicating and Handling Information 1.1, 1.2, 1.3; Modelling 1	Using the Technology; Creating and Presenting Text Level A, B; Control & Modelling Level A	*Microsoft Paint*	Literacy, art	**All year groups**
Making models	1a	Knowledge, Skills and Understanding 2c, 2d, 4b, 4c; Breadth of Study 5a, 5b	Communicating and Handling Information 1.1; Modelling 1; Use information from a variety of sources and investigate how it may be presented.	Using the Technology; Creating and Presenting Text Level A, B; Control & Modelling Level B	*Microsoft Publisher*	Science, art, language	**Year 1/P2**
Words in the bank	1b	Knowledge, Skills and Understanding 1a, 1b, 2a, 2b; Breadth of Study 5a, 5b	Communicating and Handling Information 1.1, 1.2, 1.3; Use information from a variety of sources and investigate how it may be presented.	Using the Technology; Creating and Presenting Text Level A, B	*Microsoft Publisher*	Literacy, art	**Year 1/P2**
Look around	1c	Knowledge, Skills and Understanding 1a, 1b; Breadth of Study 5a, 5b, 5c	Communicating and Handling Information 1.1; Use a variety of ICT equipment and software. Explore the use of computer systems in everyday life. Examine and discuss their experiences of ICT, and look at the use of ICT in the outside world.	Searching and Researching; Communicating and collaborating Level A	*Microsoft Publisher*	IT, art	**Year 1/P2**
Labels for everything!	1d	Knowledge, Skills and Understanding 1a, 1b, 2a, 2d; Breadth of Study 5a, 5b, 5c	Communicating and Handling Information 1.1, 1.2; Use a variety of ICT equipment and software.	Using the Technology; Creating and Presenting Text Level A, B	*Microsoft Word*	Literacy, science	**Year 1/P2**
Follow me!	1f	Knowledge, Skills and Understanding 2a, 2b, 2d; Breadth of Study 5a, 5b, 5c	Communicating and Handling Information 1.1, 1.3; Modelling 1; Use a variety of ICT equipment and software. Explore the use of computer systems in everyday life.	Control & Modelling Level A	*Microsoft Publisher*	Maths, IT, language	**Year 1/P2**
Looking at text	2a	Knowledge, Skills and Understanding 2a, 3a, 4a; Breadth of Study 5a, 5b	Communicating and Handling Information 1.1, 1.2, 1.3; Use information from a variety of sources and investigate how it may be presented.	Using the Technology; Creating and Presenting Text Level A, B	*Microsoft WordPad, Microsoft Word*	Literacy	**Year 2/P3**
Picture this	2c	Knowledge, Skills and Understanding 1a, 2a, 3a; Breadth of Study 5a, 5b	Communicating and Handling Information 1.1; Use information from a variety of sources and investigate how it may be presented.	Using the Technology; Creating and Presenting Text Level A, B	*Microsoft Paint*	Art	**Year 2/P3**
Animated books	All aspects	Knowledge, Skills and Understanding 1b, 2a, 2b 3a; Breadth of Study 5a, 5b	Communicating and Handling Information 1.1; Use information from a variety of sources and investigate how it may be presented.	Using the Technology; Creating and Presenting Text Level A, B	*Microsoft PowerPoint*	Literacy	**All year groups**

File handling and desktop management

Classroom organisation is a vital element of being an effective teacher. Children normally have books or folders in which to record their progress: they can start a piece of work, you can review it with them, they can redraft it and make corrections. You then have a record of the child's achievement and of your input as a teacher. The work will show where the child started from and where they are now; it will be dated, contain formative comments, show progression and any advances the child has made in completing the activity.

Can we recreate this same good practice using the computer? If a child is using a CD-ROM for maths practice how do we record their achievements and weaknesses? Can we have a system by which pupils can save their work and return to it at a later date? Some integrated learning programs have a built-in record-keeping system which will track a child's progress and allow work to be saved, but more often than not this feature is not available. This can be rectified simply by using features within the *Windows* operating system. Using the approach described here you will be able to create a learning environment that is flexible and allows you to record children's achievements and progression in ICT, however it is used across the curriculum.

Keeping track of these files and keeping the classroom computer in good working order, though, can be a difficult task at times. With a little bit of knowledge and some basic preparation, this can be simplified a great deal. This chapter aims to introduce some of the principles of storing information on a computer, and suggests some ways of keeping the classroom computer up and running with the minimum of fuss.

☐ Looking through *Windows*: the basics

The desktop

The screen you see when *Windows* has loaded is called the 'desktop'; it is here that all the work you do on a computer takes place. The bar along the bottom is called the 'taskbar'. Using the taskbar you can switch between a number of different programs, and access the 'Start' button which activates the *Start* menu from where you can run most of the day-to-day operations you would need to on a computer.

On to the desktop you can place a number of things: programs, 'shortcuts' to programs, files and folders. Each of these is represented by an icon, and can be clicked on with the mouse to run the program or open the file.

A File	New Folder	Internet Explorer	Shortcut to 3½ Floppy (A)
File	Folder	Program	Shortcut

Know your mouse

The mouse is a quick way of interacting with your computer. Moving an on-screen cursor, you can drag, move or change the way files are organised on the screen. Most PC mice have two (or sometimes more) buttons; you will need to use both, as each performs different functions.

Left button:
☐ a single-click will select something
☐ single-click and hold to highlight or drag an item
☐ double-click to run programs or open files.

Right button:
☐ a single-click on an icon, screen or word will make a menu relating to that object appear.

Skills practice

Try familiarising yourself with the actions of the mouse and its buttons. This is also a good set of skills for children to learn.

Left-click on an icon – this will select the icon. Then double-click on the same one. This will make something happen, depending on the

Right-click on an icon to bring up a pop-up menu of options.

type of icon you have double-clicked: a program will run, or a file or folder will open

Lastly, try right-clicking on an icon: a properties menu will appear. The kind of menu that appears will depend on the icon you have selected. Most elements of *Windows* will have a properties menu associated with them that can be accessed by right-clicking. This will provide a list of common actions that you can perform on this item. This includes not just icons, but the taskbar, 'Start' button and the desktop itself.

The taskbar

The taskbar is usually found at the bottom of the desktop. When programs, folders or files are opened they appear on the taskbar, and you can switch between a number of programs that are open at once. The taskbar has its own properties; right-clicking on a blank part of the taskbar will bring up a menu where you can customise its appearance.

The taskbar can be moved and made bigger. You may have a need to do this, but normally the taskbar along the bottom of the screen is the best option. Occasionally children (or teachers!) may accidentally move or change its size, which can be frustrating and confusing, so it is useful to know how to put the taskbar back to the size and position you want.

Moving the taskbar

Left-click and hold on a blank area of the taskbar, then drag it to the left side of the screen: the taskbar should run down the side of the desktop. Repeat, returning the taskbar to the bottom of the screen. Try moving the taskbar to the right and top of the screen.

Resizing the taskbar

Move the mouse over the edge of taskbar where it meets the desktop. The cursor should change to a double-headed arrow: ↕. Click with the left mouse button, hold and drag the cursor up. This will increase the height of the taskbar. Repeat and return the taskbar to its original size.

Customising your computer

The desktop itself also has its own properties – you can change most aspects of its appearance to suit your own tastes. Right-click on a blank part of the desktop and a menu will appear with some options. Select 'Properties' and you will see this 'Display properties' box. (This screenshot was taken from *Windows NT*, your version of *Windows* may show a slightly different set of options, but the principles will be the same.)

Changing the wallpaper

The wallpaper is the background to your desktop. It could be a pattern, your school colours, or related to your current topic. Click on the 'Background' tab in the 'Display properties' box and choose a wallpaper from the list, or browse for another image file on your hard drive. Change the display options, and when you are happy with the effect click 'OK'.

Using children's own work as wallpaper

Seeing their work displayed on the computer can be a great motivator for young children, and is easy to set up:

Open *Paint* (this application comes with *Windows* and can be found by clicking *Start > Programs > Accessories*) and let the children create some artwork.

Once they have drawn a picture, or used one of the files that accompany this book, save their work by clicking *File > Save* (make sure you remember where you choose to save the work).

Click again on *File,* you will see two more commands: 'Set as Wallpaper (tiled)' and 'Set as Wallpaper (centered)'. Select the second option and close *Paint*. The picture will now be set on the desktop.

This feature can be used to display a variety of children's work, and can be changed often. They could draw pictures based on various festivals such as Christmas or Diwali, or faces to give the computer a 'personality'. Paintings could be scanned if you have the facilities.

Changing the screensaver

Screensavers were originally designed to prevent computer screens being damaged, by displaying a continuous image when the computer was not being used. They are good fun to experiment with and can be a useful display feature.

To change your screensaver, open the 'Display properties' box and click on the 'Screensaver' tab. There are many options; 'Scrolling marquee' is a good choice for the classroom.

Select 'Scrolling marquee' and click 'Settings' to go to the screensaver options box. In the text box type the text you want displayed. This can be a list of words that children are learning for spelling, a message or rule you want the children to remember, or even birthday wishes – you could devise a list as a class. Click the 'Format text' button and choose a font and text size. You can also experiment with text and background colours and the speed at which the text scrolls. Once you are happy with the settings click 'OK'. Now when the computer is not being used it will display your message, illustrating that computers can display information.

Using and experimenting with these techniques you will be able to make the computer in the classroom look how you want and undo any modifications pupils make.

File handling

In *Windows*, files are stored in folders which, like their paper equivalents, can be named, deleted, moved and stored within other folders. By creating a filing system on your computer's desktop children can have their own folder just like they have their own book or drawer. They will be able to save work in it, or you can put work there for them to complete.

Note that the following file management system is intended to be used on standalone machines in the classroom. Its effectiveness is reduced when used over a network or with additional commercial add-ons to *Windows*. If in doubt, check with your ICT Co-ordinator.

Folders

Right-click on a blank area of the desktop. From the menu that appears, point to 'New'; a further menu will appear. Choose 'Folder', and a new folder will appear on the desktop.

Double-click your new folder. It will open up a window showing the contents of the folder. In the top right-hand corner you will see three buttons. These are common to all windows, and allow you to change the appearance of the window. Their functions are:

Minimise:
Shrinks the window to the taskbar, but keeps the window available so you can do other tasks at the same time.
Maximise:
Toggles between a small window and a full-screen view of the window.
Close:
Closes the window.

To rename your folder, right-click on the icon: a menu will appear. Choose and select 'Rename'. Under the folder, the

Arrange Icons ▶
Line up Icons

Paste
Paste Shortcut
Undo Delete

New ▶   Folder
               Shortcut
Properties
               ACDSee Image Sequence
               Briefcase

               CorelDRAW 7.0 Graphic
               Portfolio Catalog Document
               InDesign Document
               PageMaker Publication
               Adobe Photoshop Image
               Microsoft Word Document
               Corel TEXTURE Document
               Text Document
               Microsoft Data Link
               Wave Sound
               WinZip File

name label will change to a flashing cursor. Click inside the box and use the BACKSPACE key to delete the words New Folder. Type a name of your choice and press RETURN to confirm.

You can delete the folder in a number of ways. You can right-click on the icon, then choose 'Delete', answering 'Yes' when asked to confirm. Alternatively, left-click on the icon, hold and drag it to the Recycle Bin on the desktop.

Any file, folder or program can be deleted. It will always be sent first to the Recycle Bin, and you will always be asked 'Are you sure?' To delete something permanently you have to empty the Recycle Bin, so for children to delete something they would have to do it twice in two different ways. This helps stop items being deleted accidentally.

If, though, you delete a folder by mistake, all is not lost! You can undelete files and folders by double-clicking the Recycle Bin icon. This will open up a window, and you should see your folder in the list of deleted files. Right-click on it, and a menu will appear. Choose 'Restore', and the folder will return to the desktop. (In *Windows 95*, an empty folder that is deleted will disappear; only its contents remain in the Recycle Bin and can be restored.)

Recycle Bin

Files

Some files, such as basic text or graphic files, can be opened by a number of different programs. In this case, you could create a file in one application, but when you double-click on it, it will open in a different application. For example, if you create a document in *WordPad* and also have *Word* on your computer, double-clicking a *WordPad* file will open by default in *Word*. Graphic files can also cause problems as many applications can open many different types of files. Thus, a .bmp file made in *Paint* might open in another application, because .bmp files have a different default association with another program. These associations can be changed, though, so you know which files open up with which application.

Changing the program associated with different file types

To change the file associations, open up the 'My computer' window, then choose *View > Options*. Click on the 'File types' tab, and in the list of file types, choose the one you want to change and click 'Edit'. The 'Actions' tab shows a list of things that you can do to a file of that type: you want to change how it opens, so click on 'Open',

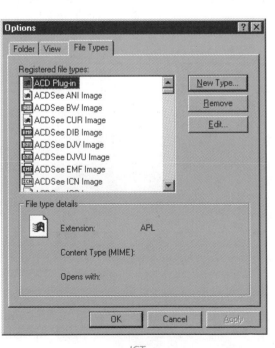

then the 'Edit' button. You can now change the settings for 'Application used to perform action'.

To find the program you want to open these files with, use the 'Browse' button. This will display a window showing the folders on your computer. Locate the program you wish to use to open the files of this type (these are normally kept in a folder called 'Program files'), then double-click the program, and choose 'OK' to complete the file association.

Practice activity

Create a folder on the desktop and name it 'Teacher'. Repeat, making five children's folders, naming them, for example, Child 1, Child 2, and so on. (Later you will need to do this for all the children in your class.) To organise the folders right-click on the desktop, select 'Arrange icons' from the properties menu and click on 'Auto Arrange': this will automatically line up all the icons on the desktop. If an icon or folder is moved it will automatically return to the left of the desktop.

Now you need to place an activity in each folder for the children to complete. Start *WordPad* (click *Start > Programs > Accessories > WordPad*), which is a simple word processor that is a standard part of *Windows*. When it is open, type a simple instruction, such as Type your name. Click on *File > Save as*. The dialogue box as shown below will appear.

Teacher

Child 1

Child 2

Child 3

Child 4

Child 5

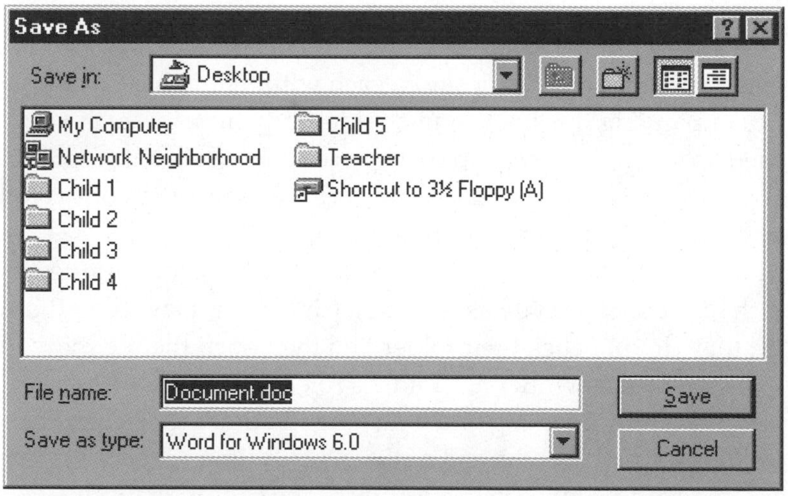

Look at 'Save in' across the top, and click on the down arrow: ■. Choose 'Desktop': you should see the folders you have created in the window below. Double-click your 'Teacher' folder to open it up, then type a filename (for example, myname) and click 'Save'. Close *WordPad*.

To test the file, double-click your 'Teacher' folder on the desktop. The folder will open and you should see the file you created inside.

File handling and desktop management

Double-click your file; it should open in *WordPad*. Now close *WordPad*, but leave the folder open so that you can see the file.

To copy this file to every child's folder, make sure you can see the folders you wish to copy the file into, as well as the open window containing the file itself. Click once on your file to select it, then press and hold the CTRL key. Click on your file, hold and drag with the mouse: you will see a 'ghost' of the file. Place this on top of one of your destination folders (you will know it is in the correct position when the folder darkens as it is selected). Release the mouse button to copy the file. Double-click on the folder to see a copy of your work in the folder. Repeat for the other children's folders.

Teacher

Child 1

Hold down the CTRL key when moving an icon to make a copy of it.

It is possible to copy many files at once to each child's folder. To select a number of files, hold down the CTRL key as you select the files, then keep it pressed as you drag the files to their new location. You can use this approach when copying files from the CD that accompanies this book: an activity file can be copied to every child's folder in the class.

When you are confident with this process, you can make folders and prepare work for the whole class quickly and easily.

In practice, this system will allow children at the computer to open their folder, and then the file they have been instructed to work on, quickly and easily – in two double-clicks they can be working on a task. You can now organise use of the classroom computer by having a rota.

Suggested organisation

So, you have 30 folders on the desktop, each with files copied from the CD accompanying this book, and a folder for yourself which you have copied as well. This gives up to 90 pieces of work that you plan to cover over the next three weeks. How does this work with only one computer and a limited amount of time?

Child 1 and Child 2 are first to start work. They have ten minutes to do as much of the first activity as they can. Child 1 starts work at the computer; they double-click their folder and then open the file they have been instructed to work on. Child 2's role is only supportive, helping with spelling, advising and watching the timer (this could be a clock or an egg timer). At the end of the allotted time, Child 1 saves their work and Child 2 takes their position at the computer, with Child 3 now in a supportive role. This continues throughout the day or week until all the children have had their turn. In the meantime you can look at each child's work, which the computer has automatically timed and dated, and make judgements about what they need to do next. Are they ready to move on? Do they need to complete the task? Are they making mistakes? Do they need more practice? Once you have made your assessment you may wish to record this progress and speak to the child, giving them feedback.

Before they next work on the file, make a copy of the first draft and keep it somewhere safe (maybe in a 'Progress' folder within the child's own folder), so they can work on the original again. You now have a record of their work before and after revision, and therefore a record of their development and a measure of the success of your input. You can then save the completed work alongside the first draft with its file name as formative comment: **Can now use the mouse more effectively.bmp**, as file names can be up to 256 characters long. Gradually, work will build up in the children's folders, and will become a complete record of their progress, showing the applications and skills they have used in ICT across the curriculum. Selected pieces of work can be printed out and placed in books or used for display.

Using a system such as this you can make far more effective use of the classroom computer, cutting down on printing and therefore printer problems, and providing a complete record of each child's ICT achievements.

The system can be modified to accommodate group work, with each group having their own folder, or adapted to take into account more than one computer, with each child having a particular computer on which they work. Machines could be given specific tasks, say one to run a maths practice CD-ROM, and another for children to work in the way outlined here.

1 : Introducing mouse control

☐ Project overview

Project	Subject link	ICT objective
A-maze-ing	Literacy (Control)	Developing control of the mouse
Practise your ABCs	Literacy (Handwriting)	Using the mouse to draw on the screen
Feast your eyes	Art	Creating pictures using a drawing package

◉ CD resources

The files for these activities are located in subfolders inside the 'Introducing mouse control' folder on the CD that accompanies this book. All the files will open in *Microsoft Paint*, which comes as standard with all versions of *Windows*, and can usually be found by clicking *Start > Programs > Accessories > Paint*.

The files you will need are: **Maze1.bmp**, **Maze2.bmp**, **Maze3.bmp**, **Maze4.bmp**, **Maze5.bmp**; any of the files **A.bmp** to **Z.bmp**; and **Eyes.bmp**.

The components required to create the maze activities as described in the Workshop sections are all stored in the 'Workshop components' folder on the CD.

Vocabulary and definitions

Brush (or paintbrush): tool used to make marks on screen similar to a real paintbrush.

'Click and drag': used to select and move an object, by holding the left mouse button down and moving the mouse so the on-screen object follows.

Double-click: two clicks in quick succession of the left mouse button, usually to launch an application or open a file directly.

Left mouse button: pressed to make something happen, such as to select or use a tool.

Mouse: device held in the hand and used to control the on-screen pointer.

Pointer: used to move around the screen and select items.

Single-click: one quick click of the left mouse button, to select an object or confirm an action.

Toolbar: a collection of tools that are available for use in the program.

Tools: functions used to create items on the screen.

Introducing... mouse control!

In this chapter, children will gain an understanding that the computer's mouse controls the pointer that can be seen on the screen. They will discover that the pointer tells the computer what to do and how to do it. It is important that children develop confidence when working with computers; knowing how to control the movement of the pointer with the mouse is the first, but possibly the most important, stage in developing this confidence.

Using a simple program called *Paint*, which comes as standard with any *Windows*-based computer, children will develop this confidence, and their control skills by using the mouse. They will have the opportunity to select appropriate drawing tools and become familiar with using the left mouse button for selecting and moving the on-screen pointer, using the paintbrush tool to paint their way through a series of mazes, around obstacles and over letter outlines. All of these activities will help to develop the skills needed to control the mouse and to produce steady, smooth movements. These activities will also help develop hand–eye co-ordination, recognition and forming of letters and matching colours, but most of all it will help extend concentration levels and try to develop their patience!

It is important that children are taught to treat the computer and mouse with respect. The equipment can withstand a great deal, but it is best to get children used to treating it carefully, gently manoeuvring the mouse rather than yanking it, and by firmly pressing the buttons but not banging them. Safety is an important issue when working with computers, so it is necessary to explain that the computer uses electricity to work and they must not use water near it or near the keyboard, highlighting that water and electricity are very dangerous when mixed together. Consult your school policy on whether children are allowed to turn computers on and off, and about supervision. Another point worth noting is that magnets can also interfere with the working of the computer, possibly leading to data loss or permanent damage to your computer, so make sure you keep them well away as well!

It may be useful to note that children may not all use the mouse with the hand that they use to write. Some left-handers may use the mouse with their right hand, and the other way around. It is important for children to feel comfortable when using the mouse.

Children should be encouraged to become familiar with using a mouse by experimenting to see what marks they can make on screen.

Skills practice

The children will need to use the index finger on their favoured hand independently of the others to be able to control the left mouse button. It is a good idea to play simple games like 'Simon says' to help them get used to this – try using commands such as 'Simon says... wiggle your index finger like me', or showing the children how to curl all their other fingers up and wiggle only the index finger. Some children will find this very difficult and it will take lots of practice to develop their control; commands such as 'Simon says... tickle your head with your index finger', or '...scratch the end of your nose', or '...wiggle your index finger up your arm like a worm' may help.

Other skills the children will need to become familiar with are 'a single-click of the mouse' and 'a double-click of the mouse'. These are commands that will be used in later chapters, but it will be useful to integrate them into the 'Simon says' game from the start. Try commands such as 'Simon says... bend your index finger once' (as if clicking the mouse button in the air), '...bend your finger twice ...now quickly', or 'bend your index finger and tap your nose once ...now twice'. These sorts of commands can be used for tapping any part of the body as long as the children practise bending their finger as if they were clicking the mouse, but don't play for too long as fingers will quickly start to ache! Playing games like this daily will help children quickly gain the strength they need to use the mouse with confidence.

Projects

A-maze-ing

Introduction

These activities have been designed to develop young children's mouse control skills. They will have the opportunity to move the mouse and click the left button to draw a line through a simple maze. The skills needed to complete this activity are similar to those needed to master basic pencil control.

ICT objectives

❑ To be able to use the mouse with a certain degree of control.

❏ To learn about some of the safety issues involved when working with computers.

Resources

You will need: access to *Microsoft Paint;* copies of the files **Maze1.bmp**, **Maze2.bmp**, **Maze3.bmp**, **Maze4.bmp** and **Maze5.bmp** from the CD; coloured stickers; photocopies of all the maze activities (print them out then photocopy them); crayons, pencils and pens.

What to do

A good starting point for this lesson would be a class discussion about using the mouse – try taking the bottom off a mouse to show the children that there is a ball inside that slides around. Show them that this ball tells the pointer which way to move.

Next, initiate a discussion about mazes. What are they? Where can we find them? Who's been in one, or followed one? Talk about the different kinds of mazes that we can find, such as those on paper, or made from plants and trees. Make sure the children know that the point of a maze is to get from the start of the maze to the end without getting lost.

Tell the children that you are going to set them a challenge. Open a copy of **Maze1.bmp** and show them the simple maze. Explain that they must use the computer mouse to show the real mouse how to get to the cheese... but they must try not to touch the sides!

Say that they will need to use one of the mouse buttons to help them, and stick a sticker of an open eye on the left mouse button so the children know which one to use. (You could stick a closed eye on

Stickers on the most-used parts of the computer keyboard and mouse can help children identify functions more quickly.

the right button.) Now look at what they need to do to draw their way through the maze. Show the children how to select the paintbrush by moving the pointer over to the picture of the paintbrush on the toolbar at the side, then clicking the left mouse button. Once selected, a choice of brush sizes will appear underneath. Choose the largest size as it is the easiest to control. Now you need to choose a paint colour. Click with the left mouse button on a colour from the palette at the bottom of the screen.

1 : Introducing mouse control

Then demonstrate the activity. Move the pointer to the start of the maze, then click the left mouse button and, still holding the left button down, draw your way through the maze with the mouse – you should leave a trail behind you.

Try and complete the maze in one smooth movement, then set the children the challenge of doing the same.

At the computer

Open a blank copy of **Maze1.bmp** for the children, and revise with them how to select the paintbrush tool, its size and the colour of the paint. Remind them that they need to hold the left mouse button down as they draw their line, but if they let go it doesn't matter – they can just click the left mouse button again, hold it down and carry on. The aim is to get through the maze in one movement, but this will take practice – encourage them to try several times, and to see if they can improve.

Let each child try to complete the maze activity three times. They can choose any colour they like, but it is a good idea if you specify – say, red for their first attempt, yellow for their second try and green for their final attempt. This will help you to keep a record of how they have improved with practice, and it also means they can try three times to complete the same maze on the same copy of the file.

Encourage the children to practise getting from the start of the maze to the end several times to see if they improve, using different colours to compare their efforts.

Show them that if they make a mistake, they can go back a step by selecting *Edit > Undo* from the top toolbar.

Once the children have completed their maze, ask them to save the file to their individual folder. Repeat this process with the other maze activities on the CD (**Maze2.bmp** to **Maze5.bmp**) for further practice, and for challenging more or less able children. These can be completed in the children's spare time or as part of a follow-up revision lesson.

To develop mouse control skills further, children could explore the maze using a different sized paintbrush, or they could try getting through the maze without touching the sides while racing against a timer (it's not as easy as it looks!).

At their desks

The maze activities can be printed out and photocopied for the children to practise pencil control. (The same colour system could be used so that progress can easily be seen.) If some children find this activity difficult, why not enlarge the maze to A3 so they have a bigger space to work in, or reduce it in size if it is too easy? For extension, encourage the children to try and design their own mazes on paper for others to follow.

Conclusion

It would be a good idea to ask a child who has improved their mouse control skills to demonstrate this good practice to the class. Alternatively, printed examples of the children's maze work could be shared with the class and any problems that have arisen could be discussed. Remind the children of the safety issues discussed at the start of the lesson, can they remember what they were?

Adapting the idea

By inserting your own Clip Art images, and drawing appropriate items with the tools in *Paint*, you can create exciting activities for the children to explore that are related to your current topic work in class. See the workshop section on page 35 to see how you can do this.

   Why not try:
❏ Using the shape tools (such as rectangles or ellipses) to create a maze like **Maze4.bmp**, or to place obstacles in the path of the maze?
❏ Using the curved line tool to create bendy mazes?
❏ Making easier or harder mazes with lots of different paths for the children to explore?

Practise your ABCs

Introduction

This activity is designed to help children practise letter formation as well as developing their mouse skills. The whole alphabet is provided on the CD, so you can choose to concentrate on letter forms that are appropriate to your literacy work.

ICT objective

❏ To be able to control the movement of the mouse with growing accuracy.

1 : Introducing mouse control

Resources

You will need: access to *Microsoft Paint*; copies of the alphabet files **A.bmp** to **Z.bmp** from the CD appropriate to your lesson; photocopies of the letter files; crayons and pencils.

What to do

Open a copy of one of the letter files on the CD, and show the children how, by using the paintbrush tool as in the previous activity, to copy the shape of the letter. Start with the outline on the left. Point to the first green dot, click and hold the left mouse button, and trace the shape of the letter with the mouse, stopping when you reach the red dot. Repeat this process for the other two letter forms, first joining the dots and then creating the shape unaided.

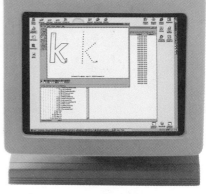

At the computer

Open a copy of one of the letter files from the CD for the children at the computer. Working individually, encourage them to select the paintbrush tool as before, to choose a light-coloured paint to draw with and to draw the shape of the letter by following the outline on the left. Remind them to try and complete this in one movement, and that they can undo any mistakes they make. Once they have mastered this, try joining the dots, then drawing the shape unaided.

When the letter form has been completed, save the file to the child's individual folder for them, or print it out to stick in their book as a record of what they can do.

Children can complete different letter forms according to their abilities, and more able children can attempt more than one letter in their allocated time.

At their desks

Print out copies of the letter files from the CD and photocopy them for the children to practise their handwriting skills. They can use a variety of colours to practise writing in different colours and sizes.

Conclusion

Examples of children's work can be placed on the wall and each letter read aloud or traced in the air to reinforce the letter shapes and formation. Choose a few children to come to the front of the class and describe in their own words how they drew the letter on the screen – it will be interesting to hear the activity described through the words of a child. Finally, the safety issues discussed earlier in the chapter can be highlighted again to ensure that all children are aware of the dangers involved when using a computer.

Adapting the idea

❑ As an extension exercise, try using the sample letter forms on the CD to create a document for each child that contains the letters of their name. They can practise overwriting this as well as using the mouse to write their name freely. The whole alphabet is in the 'Practise your ABCs' folder on the CD, and there are Clip Art images in the 'Workshop components' folder that you can insert into *Microsoft Word*.

❑ Try using *Paint* to allow children to write their names freehand using just the paintbrush tool and the mouse. They could use different colours and brush sizes to practise writing their name. The results could be printed out and used as badges or coathanger labels.

Feast your eyes

Introduction

This is a simple activity that can be used with most lessons. The focus can easily be changed to suit your current topic work, for example creating a wolf for a Literacy Hour lesson on Little Red Riding Hood.

Once the children have mastered the techniques of mouse control, drawing lines and changing colours, they can develop these skills further with a simple yet fun activity.

ICT objectives

❑ To be able to control the mouse with confidence.
❑ To be able to select and use simple tools within a graphics package.

Resources

You will need: access to *Microsoft Paint*; copies of the file **Eyes.bmp** from the CD; photocopies of **Eyes.bmp**; pens, crayons, pencils and collage materials.

What to do

The 'Flood fill' tool (highlighted) can create large blocks of colour easily.

For this activity the children will need to be able to 'fill' a shape with colour. You may want to demonstrate this to the class before they start the activity.

Show the children a blank copy of **Eyes.bmp**. Demonstrate how to select the 'Flood fill' tool, then how to choose a colour from the colour palette. Using the mouse, move the pointer over the area you want to fill with colour and click once with the left mouse button. If any mistakes are made, select *Edit > Undo* and try again.

Tell the children that they are going to use this new skill, and those that they have already learned to create a funny face based on the topic work they have been doing.

1 : Introducing mouse control

At the computer

Open a blank copy of **Eyes.bmp**
from the CD before the children
start this activity. Encourage them
to use the drawing and filling tools
and the skills they have learned to
draw eyelashes, noses and ears on
the face, choosing an eye colour
and even creating a pair of glasses!
Let their imaginations run wild!

   The completed faces can then be
named, writing a name on the picture using the paintbrush tool, and
printed out or saved to the child's folder.

At their desks

Try printing out copies of **Eyes.bmp** so that children can design their
faces on paper before working at the computer. Encourage them to
use collage materials to add to their faces, and use these as a display.
They can then try to recreate these designs on-screen, and compare the
two faces.

Conclusion

Encourage the children to compare their paper faces with the ones
they created at the computer. They can stick things onto their paper
faces – can they do this on the computer? Can they create 3-D images
on the computer? How can they get rid of mistakes on the paper
faces? Discuss the differences between the two: the children may find
that it is difficult to add details at the computer but much easier to rub
out mistakes!

Adapting the idea

Try creating other objects for the children to draw and fill in, such as
animals or houses. Why not try making:
❏ A seaside background, encouraging the children to write their name
in the sand?
❏ A ladybird shape, encouraging the children to fill the spots with the
right colours? (This activity could be linked to maths, asking 'How
many spots?'or 'Draw two more spots: how many are there now?' and
so on.)
❏ A caterpillar, where the children could fill in the missing colours
and legs?
❏ A dot-to-dot activity, where you create the dots and the children
join them up and fill them with colour?

Workshops

How to create your own maze

Resources

You will need: access to *Microsoft Paint*; Clip Art images for your maze (the images used in the activities on the CD are available in the **'Workshop components'** folder).

What to do

You can create your own themed maze activities quite simply with some Clip Art, a copy of *Paint* and a little patience. Start off by opening *Paint* and selecting *File > New*. You will see a blank canvas.

Choose the 'Line' tool, then change the thickness of the line from the menu below the tools (a thick line is easier to draw with!).

Change the colour of your line by picking a colour from the palette at the bottom of the screen.

To create a line click and hold the left mouse button where you want the line to start, then drag the pointer to the desired length while still holding down the left mouse button. It is difficult to create a straight line this way, so try holding the SHIFT key while you draw your line; this will keep the line horizontal or vertical. Now design yourself a maze. If you make a mistake it can easily be undone by selecting *Edit > Undo* from the top toolbar.

Consider the children's abilities: if this is their first experience you may want to create a simple maze, but more complicated mazes can challenge more able children. Try including more turns, closer lines and even shapes such as circles – these will extend the children's hand, eye and mouse coordination.

If you want to add Clip Art to the maze, open up the picture you want in another copy of *Paint*. Make sure it is the right size to include in your maze (if it's not, select *Image > Stretch/Skew*, and input smaller values in the 'Stretch' boxes to shrink the image until it's the right size). Choose the 'Marquee' tool and draw a box around the picture, then select *Edit > Copy* before closing this additional copy of *Paint*. In the copy of

Paint showing your maze, select *Edit > Paste* to add the picture to the maze, and position it as you wish by 'clicking and dragging' with the mouse.

Once you have created your maze, save the file to disk and/or transfer it to your teacher's folder. Your finished activity could look like that in the picture.

How to create your own set of eyes

Resources

You will need: access to *Microsoft Paint*.

What to do

If you want to create your own template for children to customise, as in the 'Feast your eyes' activity, you can do so very simply with a copy of *Paint* and some basic shapes.

Open a copy of *Paint* and select *File > New* to work on a blank canvas. Using the shape tools at the bottom of the toolbar, draw some outlines of eyes that can be filled in by the children.

Position the pointer where you want the corner of the shape to be, then click and hold the left mouse button, dragging the mouse to where you want the shape to end. Release the mouse button to draw the shape. Remember that your shapes don't need to be filled with colour, as that is what the children will be aiming to do – all you need to do is supply the outline.

You can change the thickness of the line of the shape, or draw a perfect circle or square by holding down the SHIFT key while you draw the shape. Once you're happy with your outline, make sure there are no gaps in the lines (see below) that will cause colour to 'leak' if you try to fill the shape with colour.

Save your completed template to disk, or copy it to your teacher's folder, and let the children go to town!

Use the shape tools to create colouring templates for the children.

A gap in an outline like this will mean that colour 'leaks' out of the shape when using the 'Flood fill' tool.

2 : Making models

'Click and drag': a skill used to move pictures and/or text across the screen with the mouse.

Computer simulation: using the computer to create and explore faux worlds.

Imaginary/faux: something that is not real.

Model: a real or fantasy environment created within the computer.

Real-life environment: a real environment; one that really exists and is alive.

Simulated environment: not a real environment but one inside the computer.

Virtual garden: a faux garden created inside the computer; one that is not living.

Project overview
Assembling text

Project	Subject link	ICT objective
Garden insects	Science	To use a computer to model a real situation
The bear necessities	Art	To create imaginary scenarios
Computer monster	Art, Literacy	To practise 'clicking and dragging' skills

CD resources

The files for these activities can be found in the 'Making models' folder on the CD that accompanies this book. They will open with any version of *Microsoft Publisher* from *Publisher 98* onwards. Please note that when you first open these files on a computer, you may get a message telling you that the default printer cannot be found; this is normal, and should be ignored. See the CD's 'Readme' file for more information.

The files you will need are called **Garden.pub**, **Bear.pub** and **Monster.pub**.

An introduction to modelling

Modelling in the infant classroom is a simple process by which children use computers to recreate real or fantasy situations. Playing adventure games, exploring a CD-ROM about the seashore or playing computer football are all examples of modelling. It can involve pictures, text, sound and animation: anything can be used to recreate a real (for example, the FA Cup final) or imaginary (*Toy Story*) world.

It is important, though, that children understand that the world created within the computer is not real, just a representation (or copy) of reality. In this chapter children will need to identify, and discuss, the differences and similarities between the computer simulation and the real-world situation. For example, comparing a game of computer football, played by one person controlling a whole team from the comfort of his or her seat and never getting tired, to that of a real game, with twenty-two individuals running around a muddy field in the pouring rain!

There are many CD-ROMs available that give children the opportunity to explore an imaginary world inside the computer, for example *My World* (Semerc), or *Tizzies Toy Box* (Sherston Software), or the opportunity to explore a replica of the real world, such as *Seashore* (Anglia Multimedia).

The projects in this chapter provide simple 'click and drag' activities that will give children the opportunity to explore and question different types of 'virtual' computer environments. There are also step-by-step workshops to show you how to create your own simple computer-generated environments.

These activities build upon the skills introduced in 'Introducing mouse control'. The children will need to be familiar with using and controlling a mouse, clicking the left mouse button and 'clicking and dragging' an object on the screen. These are all skills that the children practise when using most CD-ROMs, but are more specifically developed using the activities in this chapter. All these activities can be repeated several times to reinforce these skills at the same time as exploring computer modelled environments.

Some children may need to refresh their 'clicking and dragging' skills before looking at the following projects. If this is the case, begin by looking again at some of the projects in Chapter 1.

Projects

Garden insects

Introduction

This activity is modelling in its most basic form: the children can create their own 'virtual' garden by adding 'virtual' insects. There are many different locations that can be used to demonstrate the differences between real and faux environments, but the garden has been chosen for this project because it is a place with which most children are familiar. (You could combine this activity with a science lesson about environments or Minibeasts.)

ICT objectives

❏ To appreciate that computers can be used to represent a real situation.
❏ To introduce using a mouse to move objects.
❏ To begin to be able to recognise the differences between a real and simulated environment.
❏ To recognise that a computer model is not an exact replica of the original.

Resources

You will need: access to *Microsoft Publisher*; copies of the file **Garden.pub** from the CD; photocopies of **Garden.pub**; scissors, glue, writing and drawing materials, Blu-Tack, tissue paper, matchboxes and blank A4 paper.

What to do

A good starting point for this activity would be a class discussion about gardens, asking the children questions about plants and animals that live there. What do plants and animals need to live? Discuss watering in the summer, the effects of rain, and think about growing and the changing seasons.

Show the children a copy of **Garden.pub** on the computer screen. Discuss what they can see; encourage them to think carefully about the differences between the garden on the screen and a real garden. Does it grow? Does it need watering? Can we see it moving about? Do the leaves fall off the plants in the winter? Discuss different types of animals that might visit a real garden. Do they need to eat or drink? Do they grow? Encourage children to make comparisons and to understand that things in a computer do not need to be fed and watered, nor can they really move or leave the screen.

At the computer

Individual children or small groups can use a copy of **Garden.pub** to create their own 'virtual' garden by 'clicking and dragging' insects from the side of the screen on to the garden picture. They should use the mouse to select an insect by clicking on it. Once the insect has been selected a set of black squares will appear around the edges, and the pointer will change from an arrow to a 'Van' 🚚. Click and hold the left mouse button, slowly dragging the pointer onto the garden picture; the outline of the insect should follow. When the insect is in place, let go of the mouse button and the insect will be dropped into position.

The children can add as many insects as they want to their 'virtual' garden, and the insects can be moved around inside the garden until they are happy with the layout.

Once completed, save the file to the children's folder for later use. Children can then revisit their garden to allow them to practise their mouse control and 'clicking and dragging' skills.

Use the mouse to 'click and drag' items around the page.

At their desks

Children can use photocopies of **Garden.pub** as a template to create a 'virtual' garden on paper. They can cut out, colour and stick the insects onto the garden, or draw and cut out their own animals that might visit the garden, such as birds, hedgehogs or foxes.

As a class, you could design a garden environment as a collage for display. One group could make the background with paints or crayons, and the rest of the class can draw insects and animals to live in it. Cut out and stick the creatures onto the garden picture (using Blu-Tack instead of glue allows the children to move the animals around the garden).

Conclusion

Ask the class questions about the differences they found while creating their garden. Did any of the animals try to run away? Did you need to cut the grass? How many times did the bee fly off the screen? Why do you think the wind didn't make the grass move? Do you think it might rain on the garden? Encourage the children to explain in their own words the differences and similarities between the two types of garden environments.

Adapting the idea

❏ Why not create a 3-D display of your 'virtual' garden? Tissue paper could be used to create 3-D leaves and some of the animals could be glued to matchboxes to add depth. You could add a 'virtual' pond using foil, or update the garden to follow the seasons throughout the year. Printed copies of the children's 'virtual' gardens created on the computer could be included along with written work explaining in their own words the differences between the 'virtual' garden and a real one.

❑ The garden theme for this activity can easily be changed to match your topic of study – see the 'Workshop' section on page 45 for instructions on how to make your own activities.

The bear necessities

Introduction

This activity reinforces the 'clicking and dragging' skills introduced in the previous activity. The children need to be encouraged to think about the similarities and differences between dressing a real teddy and dressing the computer teddy. Try splitting the class into small groups of about four or five, giving each group a teddy and a selection of clothes, and timing them to see how long it takes to dress the bear in five items of clothing. They might find it quite difficult to get a jumper over the bear's head and pull its arms through the holes! Discuss the problems they encountered when dressing the bear. Ask which items were easy to put on and which were the most difficult.

ICT objectives

❑ To recognise the differences between computer representations of scenarios and real situations.

❑ To reinforce using a mouse to move objects.

Resources

You will need: access to *Microsoft Publisher*; copies of **Teddy bear.pub** from the CD; photocopies of **Teddy bear.pub**; scissors, glue, drawing materials, Blu-Tack, large sheets of card, sets of teddies and clothes in which to dress them and a stopwatch.

What to do

With a large teddy demonstrate to the class some of the difficulties each group encountered earlier, such as how the clothes have to be pulled over the bear's head and arms.

Show the children the teddy on a copy of **Teddy bear.pub**. Explain that they are all going to have a chance to dress this bear. Look at the clothes compared to the ones they dressed their real teddy with. Can they spot any differences? (The clothes are flat, there are no holes to put the arms through and so on.) Discuss things they think might be easier to do when dressing the computer teddy and those that might be harder. It is important not to say whether these ideas are right or wrong because they are going to investigate these when they dress the computer teddy.

At the computer

Explain to the children that they have to use the 'click and drag' technique to dress the teddy. Demonstrate the skill by selecting and moving an item of clothing onto the bear. In the garden activity, the children could place the insects in any place they wished on the garden – what would happen if they did the same when dressing the teddy? Ask the children whether they could put the shorts on teddy's head. Suggest that when completing this activity, they will need to position the garments in the correct places.

The children, either in groups or as individuals, should select items of clothing from the right-hand side of the screen and drag them onto the picture of the teddy bear. When the garment is in position let go of the mouse button and the teddy will 'wear' the clothing. The children can 'click and drag' as many items of clothing as they want to dress their 'virtual' teddy.

Once complete, save the activity to the children's folder. They can return to the file to revise their 'clicking and dragging' skills at a later date.

'Click and drag' the clothing around the page in order to dress the teddy.

At their desks

Print out a copy of **Teddy bear.pub** and photocopy it for the children to use as a template to create their own 'virtual' teddy on paper. They can cut out and stick the clothes onto the bear, or draw and cut out their own clothes. You could ask the children to design an outfit for a specific occasion, such as a party or a football match.

Ask the children to write simple statements describing the difficulties they found when dressing the real and 'virtual' teddies; they could write a brief comparison between the two bears. Which one would they like to take home? Which one would they like to cuddle?

Conclusion

Question the children again on their understanding of real and virtual situations. This may be a good opportunity to revise the ideas with children who were unsure of the differences between real and imaginary worlds at the conclusion of the last activity. Explain to the class the difference between the real and simulated teddy, and reinforce the concept that simulated things (inside the computer) are not real.

Adapting the idea

Try making a large cardboard teddy bear and asking the children to design clothes he could wear that can be attached with Blu-Tack or velcro. This could be displayed with the daily weather chart, and the clothes could be changed to suit the weather. You could even make a special set of clothes for him to wear on birthdays!

Computer monster

Introduction

The skills needed to carry out this activity are similar to the previous activities: children will need to be able to 'click and drag' objects across the computer screen. It is important in this activity for children to understand that when they create an imaginary creature on the computer they don't need to feed or look after it!

Discuss the responsibilities of having a real pet. It would need feeding and watering; it would need to be taken for a walk, to be cuddled and taught how to behave properly; it would need somewhere comfortable to sleep, somewhere to wash and somewhere to go out and play.

Now encourage the children to imagine they have a pet monster! Highlight the fact that it is imaginary and an imaginary monster doesn't need to be looked after in the same way as, say, a pet rabbit. Discuss any ideas they have about the differences between caring for these two, such as the pet rabbit's need for food.

ICT objectives

❑ To understand that computers can be used to create a range of imaginary scenarios.
❑ To create their own imaginary scenarios.

Resources

You will need: access to *Microsoft Publisher*; copies of **Monster.pub** from the CD; photocopies of **Monster.pub**; writing and drawing materials, paper, Blu-Tack, glue and scissors.

What to do

Show the children the blank outline of the monster's face on the computer screen, and explain that they are going to use this to create their own pet monster. Revise the skills needed for 'clicking and dragging' before they start this activity, and explain that they need to use this technique to move the parts of the monster's face onto the outline.

At the computer

The children, either in groups or as individuals, should work to create their pet monster's face, selecting a set of body parts from the right of the screen. Once each part has been selected, they can 'click and drag' the item onto the monster's face, letting go of the left mouse button when it is in position.

Encourage them to be creative, adding as many body parts as they want to their pet monster – remember that it doesn't necessarily have to have two eyes, a nose and a mouth!

When they are happy with their pet monster, save the file to the child's folder or print a copy out for display or discussion. As with the other activities, the file can be revisited later to allow children to develop their mouse control and 'clicking and dragging' skills.

At their desks

Give children an A3 outline of a monster's face (an enlarged printout of **Monster.pub** from the CD could be used), and ask them to try and create a variety of designs for their pet monster. Children could design their own eyes, noses, hair, mouths and teeth, and cut out and stick these onto the outline.

The children's ideas could be used to create a large class monster that can demonstrate a variety of feelings which could be changed each week, with the children writing simple poems to accompany these feelings.

Conclusion

Ask different children to explain why they chose the monster parts that they did. Are all the monsters the same? Are they real? Will that big nose be able to smell us? Encourage the children to point out that monsters like this are not real and that their computer monsters aren't either. Reinforce the idea that computers can be used to represent real and fantasy situations.

Adapting the idea

❏ Using the children's work on the computer and their paper monsters, you could create a 'monster gallery' displaying the children's pictures. Add to these descriptions written by the children about their monsters and the difference between caring for the monster and caring for a real pet.

❏ Using Clip Art of your own, you can adapt this idea so that children can create a model of almost anything with the computer! You could try: creating inhabitants for an undersea world, imagining what the inhabitants of Neptune look like, adding features to a new kind of bug discovered at the bottom of the school fields, designing a football strip for the school football team or a new school uniform.

Workshop

How to create your own modelling projects

The three modelling activities in this chapter are all very similar in structure, and this is an activity that can be adapted to tie in with almost any topic that you do in the classroom. The following step-by-step guide will show you how to create the garden insects activity, but the process will work equally well for any topic – all you need is some appropriate Clip Art and some imagination!

Many programs can be used to create a modelling activity. The examples here have been created in *Microsoft Publisher* using basic page layout techniques, but this could equally be done using any reasonably well-specified word processor.

These instructions have been written based on using *Microsoft Publisher 98*, so there may be some minor differences between this and other versions of the program. The basic principles, however, remain the same.

Resources

You will need: access to *Microsoft Publisher*; the Clip Art images supplied in the **'Workshop components'** folder of the CD.

What to do

Open *Publisher* and choose to create a 'Blank publication' when asked. Choose 'Full page' and click 'Create': this will present you with a blank A4 page on the screen.

The first thing that needs to be altered is the orientation of the page – at the moment the paper is in the 'Portrait' position (tall and thin), but it needs to be changed to 'Landscape', so it fits better on the screen. To do this click *File > Page Setup*, and click in the circle next to 'Landscape' under the 'Choose an orientation' heading. Click 'OK' and you will see that the page has changed so that it is landscape (short and fat).

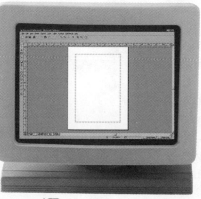

Adding the main picture

You now need to add your main picture, in this case for the image of the garden. Click on *Insert > Picture > From File* to bring up a dialogue box like the one shown here. You need to find the image you want to use, so make sure you know which folder you have put the Clip Art files in. Use the 'Look in:' drop-down menu to find the file, and make sure it's the right one with the preview window on the right. Once you've found the file (in this case, **Garden.bmp**, which is in the 'Workshop components' folder on the CD) click 'OK' and the image will be placed on the page.

To adjust the image so that it is the correct size and in the right position on the page, click on the image once with the left mouse button. Eight 'handles' will appear around the image. To resize the picture, place the pointer over one of the corner handles, so that the pointer changes to a 'Resize' icon: , then 'click and drag' the edge of the picture until it is the size you want it to be. Move the picture to the right of the page by 'clicking and dragging' the image when you see the 'Move' icon: .

You can also insert images from the Clip Art gallery if you are looking to create a different theme for your activity. Choose *Insert > Picture > Clip Art*, and find your image from the gallery that appears, then resize and position the image as before.

Creating a table

Next you need to create a table on the opposite side of the page into which you can put the objects to be added to the main picture. The table needs to have three rows and two columns. To insert a table, choose the 'Table frame tool' icon from the objects toolbar. Move the crosshair pointer +, to a corner of the place that you want the table to be, and 'click and drag' with the mouse to create a box for the table. When you let go of the mouse button, a 'Create table' box will appear. Enter the number of rows (4) and number of columns (2) required. This can be done by typing the number directly into the box, or by using the up and down arrows at the side. Click 'OK' to create your table. You can adjust the size of the table by 'clicking and dragging' one of the black rectangles at the edges of the table when you see a 'Resize' pointer.

To give your table a border, select your table by clicking anywhere on it. Move the pointer to the top-left corner of the table until the cursor changes to a hand and says 'Select cells', then click the left

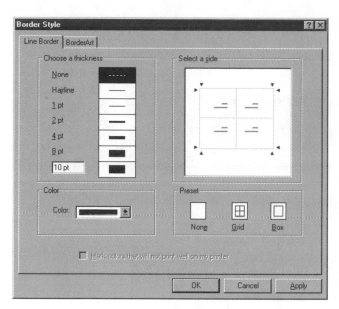

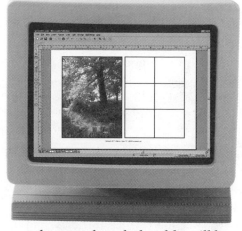

mouse button: the whole table will be selected and will turn black. Now click the 'Line/Border Style' icon on the top toolbar and choose 'More styles'. Select the 'Grid' option in the box that appears and click 'OK'. In this box you can also change the colour and thickness of the lines of the table.

Adding the final images

All you need to do now is add the Clip Art images that the children will 'click and drag' onto the main picture. You can either choose these images from the Clip Art gallery as you did before, or by inserting them individually through the *Insert > Picture > From File* dialogue box.

It is important that before you insert any Clip Art from the gallery you make sure that the table or any other part of the page has not been selected, otherwise the Clip Art will replace the selected object. To deselect objects, simply point to a blank area of the page and click once with the mouse.

Use the 'Send to Back' and 'Send Backward' options to reveal 'hidden' images on the page.

When you have inserted an image, resize it as appropriate and position it in one of the boxes of the table so that it can be 'clicked and dragged' by the children. Repeat this for all six insect images on the page.

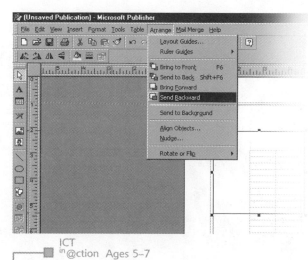

If your image disappears, don't worry! It's still there, but it has disappeared 'underneath' the table, and can't be seen. To change this, you need to send the table to the 'back' of the page, so that it is behind the images. Select the table, then click *Arrange > Send to Back*. Your picture should reappear.

Finally, if you wish, you can create a text box for the title of the work (for example, 'Garden insects'). To do this, select the text box tool ⚞, then 'click and drag' to size on the page. Change the font style, colour and size (20pt is a good size for a title) by clicking on the drop-down menus in the toolbar. Save the work in your teacher's folder and you're ready to let the children create their own models!

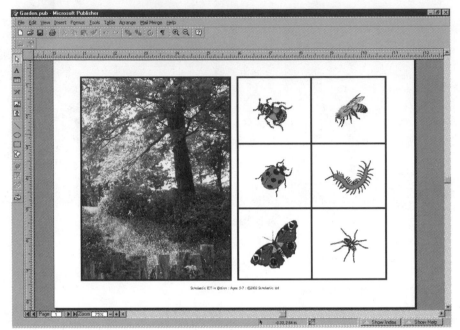

3 : Words in the bank

Vocabulary and definitions

BACKSPACE key: (often marked ⇦) used to delete a mistake made when typing. BACKSPACE will remove the character immediately to the left of the cursor.

CAPS LOCK key: sets the letter keys to type in capital letters without the need to hold down SHIFT; only to be used when writing a whole sentence in capital letters.

DELETE key: used to remove a mistake, text or picture. Can also be used to remove the character to the right of the cursor in a word processor.

SHIFT key: a key on the keyboard (often marked ⇧), which is used to create a single capital letter; hold the SHIFT key down and press any letter at the same time to create a capital.

Word bank: a group of words related to a topic created to support children's work.

Project overview

Using a word bank

Project	Subject link	ICT objective
Name that bookmark!	Literacy	Practising typing skills
Match up	Literacy	Practising 'clicking and dragging'
A monster poem	Art, Literacy	Practising 'clicking and dragging'

CD resources

The files for these activities can be found in the 'Words in the bank' folder on the CD that accompanies this book. They will open with any version of *Microsoft Publisher* from *Publisher 98* onwards. Please note that when you first open these files on a computer, you may get a message telling you that the default printer cannot be found; this is normal, and should be ignored. See the CD's 'Readme' file for more information.

The files you will need are called **Bookmark.pub, Match up.pub** and **Poem.pub**.

Using a word bank

This chapter looks at the process of dealing with simple text. The children will have the opportunity to use the computer to make a bookmark with their name on it, create a poem and use a word bank to label pictures. *Microsoft Publisher* and *Microsoft Word* are both equally good applications for manipulating text, but the activities in this chapter focus on showing how *Microsoft Publisher* can be used creatively because it allows more control over the layout of a page. Boxes, pictures and labels can be created in vibrant colours; the shape, size and style of text can be altered, and simple yet effective activities can be created quickly. The activities in the previous chapter were also developed using *Publisher*, so if you try to create your own word bank activities using the workshops at the end of this chapter you will already be familiar with some of the techniques used.

Word bank activities will also help children to build on and practise skills they have developed in previous chapters. They will continue using and controlling a mouse, using the left mouse button with confidence and 'clicking and dragging' an object or text across the screen. Once a child has mastered the skill of moving a picture around the screen, developed in the 'Making models' chapter, they can quickly transfer this skill to allow them to move text as well.

As children become more familiar with the computer they will start to use the keyboard to write simple words and phrases. The easiest thing for them to start off with is usually their name. To do this they will need to use the SHIFT key to create a capital letter for the first letter of their name, use the SPACE BAR to separate their first and second names, and the delete (BACKSPACE) key to remove any mistakes. In doing this, they will start to locate common letters on the keyboard, and begin to learn good keyboard practice.

When introducing children to word processing it is very important to teach the correct skills from the outset. One of the most common problems you need to be aware of is if a child is using the CAPS LOCK key for single capital letters rather than the SHIFT key. Children are also keen on using the SPACE BAR, and will often put more spaces into their work than they need. Once a child has got into bad habits it is very difficult to retrain them, so try to ensure good practice from the outset.

Children should be encouraged to become familiar with the basic operations of a keyboard from an early age.

Skills practice

As a class, look at the computer keyboard and discuss what the children think it is used for and what familiar things they can see on it (letters, numbers). Are the letters in alphabetical order? Why do they think they are not? (The keys are arranged so that the more common keys are easier to reach when typing quickly.) Talk about the way we type: sitting up straight facing the keyboard, using our fingers to assert a soft, but firm touch to operate the keys.

The keyboard

Open a new document in *Microsoft Word* or *Wordpad* and ask a child to demonstrate this 'good practice' to the class. What would happen if we held our finger down on a key? Or if we pressed too lightly? Choose children to demonstrate these ideas to the class. Discuss safety issues with the children, explaining that they must not get water on the keyboard or the computer because they both use electricity to work and electricity and water are a dangerous mixture.

Capital letters

Having discussed the correct way to use a keyboard, say to the children that they are now going to use it to type their name. Demonstrate this by typing your own name into a blank word processor document. Highlight the importance of having a capital letter at the start of their name, and explain that to create a capital letter they must hold down two keys at the same time – the SHIFT key and the appropriate letter key. Demonstrate that just pressing the SHIFT key doesn't do anything, so they can hold this down first and then look for the letter key. It is a good idea to put a small sticker (coloured or shaped) on the SHIFT key so the children can identify it quickly. Make sure that the children don't get into the bad habit of using the CAPS LOCK key to create single capital letters.

Correcting mistakes

Next, reassure the children that it doesn't matter if they make a mistake. Show them where to find the BACKSPACE key. (Try putting a different coloured or shaped sticker on this key to help identify it.) Explain that pressing BACKSPACE once will delete a single letter, but if they hold the key down it will keep deleting letters until they let go!

Spaces

Next, highlight the importance of having a space between words so that we can read them. The SPACE bar (the longest key on the keyboard) is used to put the spaces in, but only one space is needed between words so it only needs to be pressed once. Again choose a child to demonstrate the use of the SPACE BAR, and stick a different coloured or shaped sticker on the key to help children find it.

Let the children freely explore the SHIFT, DELETE and SPACE BAR keys by letting them type into a simple word processor such as *WordPad* (this is the basic word processing program that comes with *Windows*, and can usually be found in *Start > Programs > Accessories*). Let them explore the keyboard, typing words, deleting mistakes, putting spaces between the words and practising the skills you have just demonstrated.

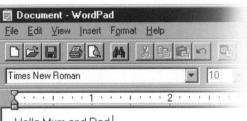

WordPad is a good, simple word processing package to allow children the freedom to develop emergent typing!

Projects

Name that bookmark!

Introduction

This simple task gives children the opportunity to use the keyboard to type their name, and would be a good activity to accompany a lesson focusing on capital letters.

ICT objective

❏ To become familiar with the keyboard.

Resources

You will need: access to *Microsoft Publisher*; copies of **Bookmark.pub** from the CD; photocopies of **Bookmark.pub**; a large A3 picture of a computer keyboard (try making a photocopy of an actual keyboard if you can't find an image – it produces excellent results!); writing and drawing materials; sticky-backed plastic or laminating pouches and small coloured picture stickers.

What to do

Explain to the children that they are going to make bookmarks for themselves using the computer, and that they can practise their typing skills as they do so. Show the children a blank copy of **Bookmark.pub** on the computer screen, and recap on the skills they will need to use in order to add their names in the spaces on the bookmark.

At the computer

The children should work individually to create their own bookmark using a blank copy of **Bookmark.pub**. They will need to use the mouse to move the pointer inside one of the boxes on the page and click the left mouse button: a flashing line (the cursor) will appear in the box. Now they are ready to type their name, as demonstrated in the 'Skills practice' section. Remind the children to use the SHIFT key to create a capital letter, and that they can use the BACKSPACE key to correct any mistakes. When they have written their name in the first box, they can select the next box and either type in their first name again or, if they can, try typing their surname.

When they have finished, save the bookmark to the child's folder so you can print it out at a more convenient time.

At their desks

Give out printed copies of **Bookmark.pub** for children to colour in themselves. They could practise writing their first name in different colours, sizes or styles, or they could write their first and second names on the sheet and use it as a name card to keep on their desk. You could ask them to make bookmarks for other members of their family, or to write key words on them to go in a word bank.

When they have finished their bookmark at the computer, they could add colour to a printout of their work. Fold the finished work in half to produce the bookmark and laminate it (or use sticky-backed plastic) so that the children can keep them in their reading books or use them as a 'name spelling' reminder.

Conclusion

Ask a confident child to come up to the computer and type their name using the keyboard. Ask them to explain how to create a capital letter. Choosing a variety of abilities of children, ask them in turn to come up and type a capital letter of your choice. Repeat this activity until you are sure all children understand that they must hold down the SHIFT key while pressing the letter key. It is important at this stage to discourage any bad habits the children might have learned at home, such as using the CAPS LOCK key to create a single capital letter which is considered bad practice.

Adapting the idea

❏ Using a copy of **Bookmark.pub**, you could try changing the colour or size of the text (so that children can fit their full name on both sides of the bookmark). You could change the border around the text using different Clip Art so that it fits the theme of the book you are reading, for example teddy bears if the story is 'Goldilocks'.

❏ Try typing key words to put in a word bank.

❏ You could try making name badges for all staff members and frequent visitors, or birthday boy/girl tags that could be made into a necklace.

■ Match up

Introduction

This activity focuses the children's attention on the relationship between text and pictures. It allows them to use the mouse to match words and pictures, and assemble sentences based on what they can see on the screen.

It uses the same skills as have been introduced in the previous chapters, so the children now have the chance to improve their ICT skills in small steps. The words chosen for this exercise (CVC) have been selected from the *National Literacy Strategy* Year 1 Term 1 (Reception revision), but with suitable Clip Art you can change the words to any that are suitable for your class.

ICT objectives

❏ To understand that simple words can be used to identify or label an object.

❏ To begin to be able to use the mouse to 'click and drag' a word to a different position.

Resources

You will need: access to *Microsoft Publisher*; copies of **Match up.pub** from the CD; photocopies of **Match up.pub**; scissors, glue, writing and drawing materials.

At the computer

Open a blank copy of **Match up.pub** before the children start the activity. Children can try this activity individually, or in small groups or pairs if it would suit their ability.

Explain to the children that the idea of this activity is to complete the sentences on the left of the page by choosing the correct word to describe the picture from the choice of three on the right.

If you want to change the words that the children need to choose from to those you are working on in literacy time, delete them and replace them with your own selection.

First they need to identify which of the three words is going to complete each sentence. Once they have chosen the correct word they should select it by clicking on it with the left mouse button. When selected, black squares will appear around the edge and a flashing cursor will appear inside the word.

To move the word, the children need to move the pointer to the edge of the word until it changes to a van icon: 🚚. Only with this cursor can you 'click and drag' the words; if you 'click and drag' elsewhere you will select the text itself rather than move the word. When the cursor changes, click, hold and drag the word across the screen into position at the end of the sentence, then let go of the mouse button.

Repeat this for the other three sentences on the page, then save the children's work in their folder for assessment purposes.

At their desks

Give out printed copies of **Match up.pub** and encourage the children to practise adding the correct CVC words to complete the sentences. They can either write the missing words at the end of the sentence or cut the correct word out and stick it in the correct place. As an extension exercise, try blanking out the pictures before you photocopy the page for the children; then ask them to choose a word from the box and draw a picture to go with it. Less able children could simply draw a line connecting the word to the sentence.

Conclusion

When sitting with the whole class encourage the children to explain in their own words how to move an object across the screen. Choose a child to demonstrate as another describes what they are doing.

Adapting the idea

❑ The idea behind this activity can be adapted to suit your classroom work very easily by changing the choice of words, or adding your own Clip Art images based on topic work. You could integrate with work in the Literacy Hour by focusing on initial blends such as *ch, sh,* or *th*; practising word endings such as *ll, ss* or *ng*; or the long vowel phonemes *ee, oo* or *ai*. 'Click or drag' endings onto the end of words, such as 'clicking and dragging', adding *–ing* to the end of 'click and drag'. Try other familiar words such as *sing, spell* or *ring*.

❑ Try looking at grammar, encouraging the children to put full stops or punctuation marks at the end of sentences, or ordering days of the week or months of the year.

A monster poem

Introduction

Young children always find it difficult to create a poem unaided, especially one that doesn't rhyme! This activity shows how to create a simple poem by 'clicking and dragging' words to complete sentences. The children will build on the skill of being able to 'click and drag' a word to now moving a selection of words to complete a sentence.

This would be a useful activity to coincide with any lesson involving poetry writing or looking at adjectives.

ICT objectives

❑ To revise the skill of 'clicking and dragging'.
❑ To be able to create a structured poem using adjectives.

Resources

You will need: access to *Microsoft Publisher*; copies of **Poem.pub** from the CD; photocopies of **Poem.pub**; an image of a keyboard (try photocopying a real computer keyboard), scissors, glue, coloured stickers, sweet wrappers, bright-coloured paper or foil, writing and drawing materials.

What to do

Discuss the structure and content of a poem with the class. Highlight that a new line can be started for each new sentence and that adjectives are used to describe things. Together, write a class list of adjectives that could be used to describe a monster, such as smelly, scary, red and so on.

Now show the children a blank copy of **Poem.pub** on the computer screen. Encourage them to read the first part of the sentence 'My monster has...', then explain that the second part of the sentence is missing, and they should choose a sentence ending from the list on the right to describe their monster. Read each sentence ending with the children so they are all familiar with the options. Revise how to select text by clicking on it then, when the black squares appear, moving the pointer until it changes into a van and 'clicking and dragging' the text into position. Once in place, let go of the mouse button and the word will be dropped into place.

Explain to the children that they are going to use these sentence endings to create their own poems about an imaginary monster. If you have already created a monster face in Chapter 2, 'Making models', you could ask the children to think about the monster they created in that activity when writing their poems.

At the computer

The children should work in small groups or as individuals to create their poems. Mixed ability groups will allow more confident readers to support those who may struggle in this activity. The children choose the sentence endings they want and drag them across the page to complete their poem. When the poem is complete there will be three sentence endings left; the children can use these to practise using the BACKSPACE key, clicking with the mouse at the end of the remaining sentences and pressing BACKSPACE until they have been removed. Once the poems are complete, save them to the children's folders so they can be printed out at a more convenient time.

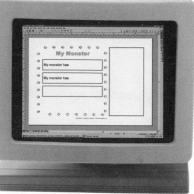

The words in the box on the right of the page can be deleted and changed for others you are working on in class if required.

At their desks

Once the sentence endings have been cleared and the poem has been printed, there will be an empty box on the right-hand side of the page. The children can use this space to draw a picture of their monster, or to create a collage using sweet wrappers and tin foil.

Alternatively, give children printouts of **Poem.pub** and ask them to either copy the sentence endings into the spaces themselves or cut and stick the typed endings into place.

All the completed poems could be put together to create a class 'Book of monster poems', or displayed along with paintings or 3-D models of monsters. The display could also include work from the 'Computer monster' activity in Chapter 2, 'Making models', and a simple explanation of the ICT skills the children have used to create their poetry and pictures. Why not include an A3 photocopy of the keyboard, with SHIFT, BACKSPACE and SPACE BAR keys highlighted and labelled?

Conclusion

Ask different children to come to the front of the class and read their poem out loud. Are all the poems the same? Why might this be? Encourage children to explain how they created their poem (by 'clicking and dragging'). Can they think of any other adjectives that could have been used?

Adapting the idea

❏ You could change the subject of the poem based on work you are doing in the classroom. Possible topics include 'Myself', 'My pet', 'Our school', 'A spider!', or any festivals you may be celebrating, such as Christmas, Easter, Diwali or St David's Day.

❏ Try encouraging the children to type their own sentence endings into the boxes, or take the activity a step further and create a short story using the same idea, giving the beginning of the sentence and asking the children to complete it. This type of activity could help children develop the idea that a story has a beginning, a middle and an end.

Workshop

▪ How to create your own bookmark

It is easy to create your own bookmark activity using Clip Art suited to work you are doing in the classroom. Many programs can be used, but this example has been created in *Microsoft Publisher.* Any reasonably well-specified word processor could do a similar job.

These instructions have been written based on using *Microsoft Publisher 98*, so there may be some minor differences between this and other versions of the program. The basic principles, however, remain the same.

◉ Resources

You will need: access to *Microsoft Publisher* and suitable Clip Art for your bookmark.

What to do

Open *Publisher*, and create a new, blank document. You will need to change the orientation of the page from 'Portrait' to 'Landscape', so the bookmarks will be long and thin when folded. To do this, click *File > Page Setup* and choose the 'Landscape' option. Click 'OK' and the page will change shape on screen.

You need to create four frames to comprise the rest of the bookmark: two that hold the borders for the front and back of the bookmark, and two to hold the text. Select the text box tool, and 'click and drag' the cursor to create the text box that is the size and shape of the top half of the page. This box will be the border for your bookmark. Click on the 'Line/Border' icon on the top toolbar ▤, select 'More Styles', then 'Border Art'; scroll through the sample images, and select the design you want by clicking on it. Click 'OK' and a border will be created around the edge of your box.

Inside this border, you need to create a text frame into which the children will type their name. This is easy: just

Use the 'Text box' tool (circled below) to create the frames for the children to type in.

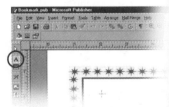

draw another, slightly smaller, text box inside the border. The text boxes can be formatted to hold text in any font, size or style. For this activity, choose an easy-to-read font and a large type size (say, 135pt) by using the drop-down menus on the top toolbar. You may also want to pick a colour for the text based on the colours of your border, but make sure that the text remains readable. Make sure you set the alignment of the text to 'Center' so that the words appear across the middle of the bookmark.

This gives you one half of the bookmark. It is easy to create the second half by copying what you have already created to the clipboard and pasting it into the lower half of the page. Choose *Edit > Select All* to highlight both text boxes at once, then click *Edit > Copy* to place a copy of the two text frames on the clipboard. They are stored here, and copies can be placed anywhere else you wish in a *Publisher* document. Deselect the two frames by clicking with the left mouse button on a blank area of the page, then click *Edit > Paste* to add another copy of the two frames to the page. Move them in to place by 'clicking and dragging' with the mouse, and you have a completed bookmark! Save the file to your teacher's folder ready for use in a lesson.

How to create your own 'Match up' activity

The other two activities in this chapter are based around a similar structure, and are again quite easy to make with your own Clip Art images.

These instructions have been written based on using *Microsoft Publisher 98*, so there may be some minor differences between this and other versions of the program. The basic principles, however, remain the same.

Resources

You will need: access to *Microsoft Publisher* and Clip Art appropriate for your activity (the images used in this chapter are available in the 'Workshop components' subfolder on the CD).

What to do

Open *Publisher* and create a new blank document, changing the orientation of the page to 'Landscape' as before.

The basic set-up of either of these activities is now simply a case of adding text and illustrations, and placing them on the page so that the children can create or complete sentences by dragging individual elements around the page. It is, therefore, important to make sure that all the parts that need moving are kept separate on the page, even if this means individual words have their own text box. Each element can be added in one of three ways.

To add text, such as a sentence ending, just use the text box tool to draw a box, then type your text into it and format it, changing the colour, size and style of the font as you wish.

You can add images either as Clip Art by clicking *Insert > Picture > Clip Art*, or other pictures by clicking *Insert > Picture > From File* as described in earlier workshops. To see how one of the activities on the screen is constructed, take a look at the file on the CD, and see how all the different parts fit together, as shown below.

The sentence beginnings have been created using a single text box.

Each picture has been inserted as Clip Art and positioned on the page.

The selection of word endings has been created from four separate boxes: one for the border, and one for each choice of word.

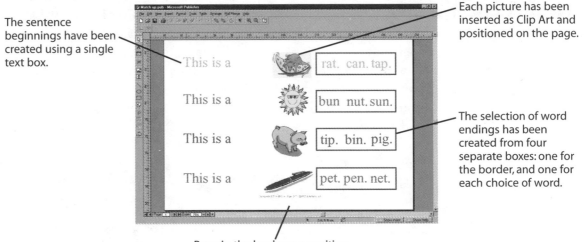

Page in the landscape position.

4 : Look around

@: part of an e-mail address
that separates the
individual user's name from
the name of their Internet
Service Provider.

CD-ROM: a circular plastic
disc used to store
information in a format that
can be read by a computer
with a CD-ROM drive.

e-mail: common name for
electronic mail: the sending
of a message from
computer to computer via
telephone lines.

Floppy disk: used to store
information in a magnetic
format that can be read by
a computer with a floppy
disk drive.

Icons: graphical symbols
placed on the computer's
desktop that can be used to
open a file or program.

Project overview

The information around us

Project	Subject link	ICT objective
Information all around	ICT, Literacy	To know and recognise that information can be presented in different forms
Storing information	ICT	Know that computers store information in different ways
No stamp required	ICT	See how computers can pass information between themselves

CD resources

The files for these activities can be found in the 'Look
around' folder on the CD that accompanies this book. They
will open with any version of *Microsoft Publisher* from
Publisher 98 onwards. Please note that when you first open
these files on a computer you may get a message telling
you that the default printer cannot be found; this is normal,
and should be ignored. See the CD's 'Readme' file for more
information.

   The files you will need are called **CD-ROM.pub**,
Computer.pub, **Disk.pub**, **E-mail.pub** and
Information.pub.

The information around us

Information is around us all the time: posters, labels and newspapers are part of everyday life. In this unit, children will explore a variety of ways in which information can be presented. They will discover that ICT (computers and other technological equipment) are useful and powerful tools for processing and communicating information.

By the end of the unit, children will be aware that information can be presented in a variety of different ways, and that it may come from a variety of sources. Before starting this chapter make a class collection of equipment that provides information today, equipment from the past and ideas for the future. Record players and old vinyl records are great for studying advances in technology when compared with a CD player and CD, and MP3 players. You frequently see old ZX Spectrum computers, cassette recorders and music boxes in junk and charity shops, so it is worth looking out for these items before you start this chapter.

It may also be useful to ask a friendly local computer company if they have any old/spare computer components (circuit boards, disk drives, wires and other circuitry) that you could use to show children and make a display of the inside workings of a computer.

© Photodisc, Inc.

Skills practice

If you have any spare or old computers in school (even BBC micros!), try setting them up in your classroom's home corner and encouraging the children to type messages on the keyboard (without the computer turned on), writing the messages on paper and sticking them to the screen. They could also draw pictures or write stories and stick these on the screen. These are simple activities, but children love having the freedom to use a computer independently, and shopping lists, letters home and class rules are frequently created! This chapter encourages children to think about the technology they encounter daily, and introduces them to the need for information to be stored and controlled.

Projects

Information all around

Introduction

This activity will encourage children to start looking at the different ways in which information is communicated, and to see what information is around them in the classroom. It will also help them to think about the ways in which this information can be sorted.

ICT objectives

❏ To recognise that information can be presented in different forms.
❏ To know that information can come from a variety of sources.

Resources

You will need: printed copies of **Information.pub** from the CD which can be used as worksheets (print one copy and photocopy enough for the whole class); examples of sources of information, such as books, maps, photographs, posters, TV listings, an alarm clock; glue, scissors, writing and drawing materials and magazines or catalogues with images of sources of information that can be used for collage.

What to do

Discuss with the class words, pictures and sounds that tell us about things and how they pass on information. Show the class a variety of such sources of information and discuss the information they are providing, for example:
❏ photographs that show us what things look like,
❏ maps or labels that show us where things are,
❏ alarms that give us warnings (or alarm clocks that tell us when it is time to get up),
❏ timetables that tell us when things are supposed to happen.
Spend a few minutes with the children looking around the classroom for places where information is given, for example signs, labels or computer icons. Encourage the children to think about the way that the information is being communicated (passed from one person to another), for example:
❏ text (handwriting, or from a computer or typewriter),
❏ sound (voice, alarms),
❏ pictures (photographs, drawings, magazine pictures),
❏ symbols (road signs or icons).

Now think about other ways of communicating information or passing on a message, such as by post, e-mail, fax or telephone. Look together at the way text is produced on a computer. Using *WordPad* type a simple message to the whole class, such as 'Make sure you work hard all day!' to highlight that computers can be used to communicate a wide variety of information.

At their desks

Using copies of **Information.pub** from the CD and your collection of objects, ask the children to put the items that communicate information into the groups listed on the worksheet, either by drawing a picture of the item on the sheet, writing its name or finding a picture of the object from a catalogue and sticking it in position. Suggest that items they find that communicate information in more than one way should go in the 'Multimedia' section, explaining that 'multimedia' means a mix of more than one way of communicating (for example a talking alarm clock that displays the time in words and also speaks to you).

Conclusion

Remind the children that information can be found in lots of different places and can be in many forms. Ask them to look around the classroom – can they find any places where information is stored or displayed? Look at books, signs, notices, tapes and so on.

Adapting the idea

❑ Try setting up areas in the classroom where the children can physically group items using the categories on the worksheet and plastic PE hoops to sort the items.
❑ Ask the children to see if they can think of more ideas by looking around their homes for more sources of information, such as a cooker timer or the symbols on a TV remote control. A large pin board divided into the same groups will allow children to pin up drawings of items they found at home.

Storing information

Introduction

This activity will show children that computers are a useful and powerful tool for processing (making) and communicating (passing on) information.

Discuss this with the children, and think about the fact that this information needs to be kept (stored) somewhere, like words are 'kept' in a book. Use this analogy to encourage the idea that information created with a computer can be stored in large quantities in the computer itself (like in a library), or on a CD-ROM (like in a set of books), or on a floppy disk (like in a single book).

Ask the children to think about what type of things they see or hear when they use the computer in school or at home. Encourage them to think of things like pictures, text (different shapes and sizes), icons, sounds and videos. They will frequently find two or three of these working at once. Explain that this is why computers are called multimedia machines, because they can do lots of things all at once.

ICT objectives

❏ To know that information can be stored in a variety of different ways.
❏ To know that sounds, pictures and words all provide information.
❏ To know that computers can store all types of information in a variety of ways.

Resources

You will need: printed copies of **Disk.pub** and **CD-ROM.pub** from the CD to use as worksheets; a floppy disk that has been taken apart before the lesson; writing materials, scissors, glue and a selection of catalogues and magazines to cut pictures from.

What to do

Show the children a real floppy disk and explain that large amounts of information can be stored on these small pieces of plastic, like in a thick book. Show the children where it fits into the computer (in the floppy drive), then create a simple sentence in *WordPad* and save it to a floppy disk while the children are watching.

Talk about how and where information is stored inside a book: we can see the words on the pages. Then discuss how they think information is stored inside the floppy disk. Where is the sentence they have just seen you save onto the disk? Show them the insides of a floppy disk (the information is stored on the floppy circle in the centre, hence floppy disk!), and say that pictures, text, sound and symbols can be stored on these disks, but we can't see the information like we could with words in a book because we are not electronic. The computer can see the information, because it can 'read' the disk!

Now show the children a CD-ROM. Point out that a CD-ROM is just like a music CD, but it holds a different kind of information; explain that the same type of information may be stored on a CD-ROM as on a floppy disk, but a CD can hold a great deal more information – up to 400 times as much as a floppy disk. Explain that a

CD-ROM could store the same amount of information as a whole set of encyclopedias: carrying one CD-ROM would be like carrying 100 big hard-back books!

At their desks

Split the class into two groups. Give each child in one group a copy of **Disk.pub**, and each child in the other group a copy of **CD-ROM.pub**. Ask the children to look through magazines and find things that they could store, or keep, on either a disk or a CD-ROM. Ask them to draw, or cut out and stick the items in the space on their worksheet. Make sure the children know that a CD-ROM can hold much more information than a floppy disk.

Conclusion

Gather the children together and ask them what things they found that could be kept on either a floppy disk or a CD-ROM. What things were the same? What big things do they think would fit on a CD-ROM that wouldn't fit on a floppy disk?

Adapting the idea

❏ Once all the children have completed the worksheet, create a giant whole-class disk made out of card displaying the parts of a disk along with the children's work. The silver protective cover could be made using silver foil or paper. The children could also draw and label pictures explaining how they think information is stored onto a floppy disk.

❏ Make your own CDs out of card, covering them with foil, holographic wrapping paper or silver spray paint to produce the shiny effect of a CD-ROM, then turn these into a backdrop for an information display.

❏ Ask the children to collect CD-ROMs that come free with magazines or Internet discs to add to a display. These could be used as mounts for children's pictures, or as clocks, coasters or spinning tops. They can also be used to create stunning mobiles (especially when placed where they catch the light), along with old floppy disks to display ICT key words such as *disk, CD-ROM, computer, monitor, keyboard*. Try putting them carefully in a tank of water, where they can create wonderful coloured patterns.

No stamp required

Introduction

Computers can be used to send information from one person to another. Sending an e-mail is a great deal faster than using post – they can reach the recipient just seconds after they are sent – and e-mails don't need a stamp! Computers can send text, pictures and sound by sending the messages down a telephone line. This lesson will demonstrate the basic principles of e-mail to the children.

ICT objectives

❑ To know that information can be communicated in manyways.
❑ To know that computers can pass information from one machine to another.

Resources

You will need: enough printed copies of **E-mail.pub** from the CD for each child; three enlarged copies of **Computer.pub** from the CD; string, writing and drawing materials.

What to do

Before the lesson starts, create a 'Virtual e-mail system' in the classroom by placing three large pictures of a computer in different parts of the room.

Colour-code the machines so that they can easily be identified, and join all the computers together by stretching string between them (to represent 'virtual' phone lines). Initially, you may want to nominate one machine to send the messages, and the other two to receive; this can be changed later in the activity.

Revise with the children the idea of communicating in a variety of ways, such as through text, sound, symbols or pictures. Explain that computers can be used as a very quick way to send messages to one another, and that you have set up a system that will let them do this in the classroom.

Say that, just like a letter sent by post, the messages or letters still need an address. As a class, decide an address for each of the computers around the room, such as redcomputer.com, bluecomputer.com and greencomputer.com. Label each computer clearly with its new address.

At their desks

Give each child a copy of **E-mail.pub,** and show them how to fold the paper in half so that the address box is on the front of the folded paper. Ask the children to think of a message they would like to send to someone at the red computer, such as 'Hi Mum, having a great day, love Fred', and ask them to write this message on the inside of the worksheet. They could also draw a picture to go with their message. When they have done this, they need to write the address of the recipient in the box on the front: To Mum@redcomputer.com, and add their own address as well: From Fred@bluecomputer.com.

Remind the children that e-mails don't need stamps, so they are ready to send. Hang the message on the line that joins the two computers, and let the message slide along the line to the red computer.

Allow children to practise writing messages and sending them between the computers in the classroom. Ask children to work in groups, each stationed by a different computer. They can write messages on blank copies of **E-mail.pub**, then 'send' them to other groups, who can open the message, read it and reply to it.

Conclusion

Discuss the children's ideas about how the messages are sent from one computer to another. They don't need to know how e-mails are sent, but they are bound to ask: simply explain that the letters are sent along the telephone wire to another computer, in the same way as their voice would be if they were talking on the phone. Remind the children that lots of different types of information can be sent – can they name any?

Adapting the idea

❑ The string lines connecting the computers don't have to be straight: they can zig-zag across the classroom until they join another computer.

❑ More than three computers could be set up as the children get the idea of messages being sent along a phone line, and you could create a virtual telephone line to another classroom or the office!

❑ Keep a supply of copies of **E-mail.pub** next to the computer so that the children can send e-mails in their own time to one another. This is a great way to encourage children to develop their emergent writing skills.

5 : Labels for everything!

Vocabulary and definitions

Label: a key word or phrase to describe an object.

Key words: a simple word to describe/ name an object.

Information: a group of words, a picture or a sound that tells us something.

Sorting: to place objects into groups with similar characteristics.

Project overview
Labelling and classifying

Project	Subject link	ICT objective
That's mine!	Literacy	To understand that objects can be labelled with information
Describe me!	Literacy	To describe and group objects with key words
A label for everything	Science, Literacy	To use labels for identification
Butterfly	Science	To use labels for identification

CD resources

These activities are located in subfolders inside the 'Labels for everything' folder on the CD that accompanies this book. All the files will open into *Microsoft Word*. They are designed to be compatible with all versions after *Microsoft Word 97*, but are not intended to work with *WordPad*. If *WordPad* opens these files rather than *Word*, please refer to the 'File handling and desktop management' chapter. If, when you open the files into *Word*, you cannot see the whole activity, select *View > Page Layout*, and then set the 'Zoom' to 'Whole Page' or 'Two Pages' as appropriate.

The files you need for the activities in this chapter are **Name.doc**, **Pencil.doc**, **Objects.doc**, **Describe.doc**, **Sorted.doc**, **Ordering.doc**, **Book.doc**, **Classroom.doc**, **Computer.doc**, **Body.doc** and **Butterfly.doc**

Labelling and classifying

In this chapter, children will have the opportunity to look at key words as a way of describing objects, and to use these to create simple labels. Labelling objects, especially in the classroom context, not only helps children to identify an object by appearance, but also helps them become more confident spellers because they are surrounded with words.

These activities will help build on word processing and 'clicking and dragging' skills developed in Chapter 2, 'Making models', and children will be able to experience working with a different program. Up until now, the activities have concentrated on using the desktop publishing package *Microsoft Publisher*. Those in this chapter have been created in *Microsoft Word* so that children can become familiar with using both packages from an early age.

It may be beneficial to explain to the children before they start these activities that they are using a different program to do the activities in. Explain that it is just like using a different book to do their work in, for example the difference between their maths and English books: they look slightly different, but both allow you to do similar things.

The two slight differences between the packages are:
❏ When clicking on a word or picture to select it, in *Publisher* black squares appear around the edge, and in *Word* a frame with white squares appears.
❏ The cursors that appear when the pointer is positioned over the edge of a word or picture ready to move it are different: in *Publisher* a van will appear and in *Word* an arrowed cross will appear.
There are other differences, but these are the only two that will affect the way the children use the two packages in any of the following activities.

Children will quickly discover that simple text can be used to identify everyday objects and pictures. They will also have the opportunity to learn that objects can be divided into groups depending on key describing words, and will be able to use the computer to create labels that will allow them to do this.

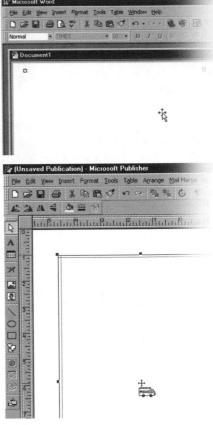

In *Microsoft Word (top)*, a selected object is highlighted with small white squares whereas in *Publisher (bottom)* the object is surrounded by small black squares.

Skills practice

Some children might need to practise typing their name confidently and refreshing their 'clicking and dragging' skills before they begin the activities in this chapter.

Children can use *WordPad* to practise writing their name. They may need to be reminded how to use the SHIFT key to create a capital letter and how to use the BACKSPACE key. To help identification, make sure that the stickers placed on the keys during Chapter 3 'Words in the bank' are still in place on the SHIFT and BACKSPACE keys, and the SPACE bar).

Practise 'clicking and dragging' skills by revising the activities **Garden.pub** or **Bear.pub** from the CD, which are described in detail in Chapter 2, 'Making models'.

Projects

That's mine!

Introduction

As children become more familiar with words they become increasingly aware of the wide range of labels, signs and posters that surround them. Try starting this whole-class lesson by discussing the variety of different kinds of text they can see in the classroom. Look at the shapes, sizes, styles and colours. Reinforce the idea that words can provide information, as discussed in the previous chapter, and encourage the children to look at how words can be used as labels to help them identify what things are called.

ICT objectives

❑ To understand that objects can be labelled with information.
❑ To revise using the SHIFT key to create a capital letter.

Resources

You will need: access to *Microsoft Word*; copies of **Name.doc** and **Pencils.doc** from the CD; photocopies of **Name.doc**; writing and drawing materials, sticky-backed plastic or laminating pouches, Blu-Tack, scissors, safety pins, a permanent marker that is suitable for writing on clothes, coathangers and string.

What to do

Encourage the children to think about labelling objects so we know who they belong to. Try telling them a simple story:

There was a class of children very much like this, but not quite as clever! They all got changed for PE, but instead of putting their jumpers on their chairs they put them in a huge pile on the floor! When they got back from PE they had a huge problem! They couldn't tell whose jumper was whose. Every child in the class (and there were 30 of them!) had all got the same blue, school uniform jumper. How were they going to find out which jumper belonged to which child before it was time to go home? Oh no, disaster!

Ask the children if they can think of a way to tell the jumpers apart. If the children suggest looking at the sizes, explain that this is a good idea but they had tried this and lots of the jumpers were all the same size! If they suggest smell (a great many infant children can smell a jumper and tell you who it belongs to!), explain that the children had thought of this idea too but because the jumpers had been in a big pile they now all smelled the same! Try to guide the children towards the idea of a name label. (If they are struggling to think of name labels, encourage them to look at their own jumper: how do they know it is theirs?)

Once the children think of using their name labels, you can finish the story:

A long time later, and after a lot of different ideas, the children had almost given up hope of finding their jumpers by home time. Then the quietest child in the class, called Fred, asked in a very quiet voice, 'Why don't we just look for the name labels in the jumpers?' Everyone was delighted because every child had their name written on a label inside their jumper! From that day on all the children decided that Fred was the cleverest boy in the whole class because he had thought of the idea (and they always put their jumpers on the back of their chairs when they got changed for PE as well!)

Ask the children if they have got their name written on a label in their jumper. Encourage them to think of other things that have their names on, such as class draws, clothes pegs, pencils, coats and bags. Explain that we label things with a name so we can quickly find out who it belongs to.

In Chapter 3, 'Words in the bank' the children had the opportunity to practise typing their name to make a bookmark. The following activity **Name.doc** gives the children another opportunity to type their name on a label, but this time they also have to think of places to put three labels, such as above their coat peg, on their class draw or perhaps as a badge on their jumper.

Show the children a copy of **Name.doc** on the computer screen and recap how to create a capital letter for the start of their name by holding down the SHIFT key while they type the first letter. Make sure the cursor is in the top box on the page, and ask a child to come and type their name into the box for you. Remind them that they can use the BACKSPACE key if they make a mistake, and that the stickers on the keyboard are still there to help them find the right keys to press.

At the computer

Working on their own copy of **Name.doc**, children need to use the mouse to move the pointer until it is over the box they want to type their name in. Once there, they should click the left mouse button once to tell the computer this is where they want to write. Encourage the children to type their first name, using the SHIFT key to create the capital letter. Tell them to repeat this in the other boxes, so that they have their name in each of the three boxes. Save the work to the child's folder and then print out at a more convenient time.

At their desks

Using a photocopy of **Name.doc**, ask children to practise writing their name in different shapes, sizes and colours for other name labels. Once their copy of **Name.doc** has been printed they could add a picture of themselves, or design a border for their label. Get them to cut out each of the three labels, laminate or protect them with sticky-backed plastic, then stick them with Blu-Tack in the required place. To make a name badge, Sellotape a safety pin to the back of the label so you can attach it to the child's jumper.

Conclusion

Gather the children together and look at the name labels they have created. Ask children to explain how they typed their name in, and if they can remember how to create a capital letter.

Adapting the idea

❑ Use a copy of **Pencils.doc** from the CD to create small name labels for the children to label their pencils. One sheet will be enough to create two labels each for a class of thirty.

❑ Why not change the size of the labels on the computer so that they fit neatly onto the children's draws or above their pegs? You can do this by 'clicking and dragging' the handles that appear when you click on the edge of the text box.

❑ With parents' permission, ask the children to write their name on the label inside their jumper using a permanent pen.

❑ Create a class mobile with the name labels. Use coathangers to suspend the labels from the ceiling in different layers, and ask the children to draw a picture of themselves on the back of the label so you can see them when the mobile spins around.

❏ A set of labels could be used to create a class graph, grouping the children's names according to different criteria (boys and girls, hair or eye colour and so on).

Describe me!

Introduction

These two activities follow on from one another, and encourage children to start to classify objects based on their key properties. They can be completed in succession, or by different groups of children.

Choose an object in the classroom and brainstorm words to describe it. Encourage description of the colour, size, shape and texture, and limit the descriptions to one-word answers (such as red, hard, square, smooth, table). Repeat this with other items until the children understand the idea of giving single key words to describe an object. Choose another object, such as a small, red, ball. Ask the children to think of three words they could use to describe it. Highlight that objects can be described using just single key words.

ICT objectives

❏ To understand that objects can be described using key words.
❏ To learn that objects can be divided into groups using key word criteria.
❏ To revise the 'click and drag' skills needed to move text.

Resources

Each activity requires a collection of objects for the children to look at and sort – these collections can be tailored you your needs if required.

Activity A

You will need: access to *Microsoft Word*; copies of **Objects.doc** from the CD; photocopies of **Objects.doc**; a variety of some (but preferably all) of the following objects: red, yellow, green and blue balls, one large and one small; red, yellow, green and blue boxes, one large and one small; red, yellow, green and blue pieces of paper, one large and one small; scissors and Blu-Tack.

Activity B

You will need: access to *Microsoft Word*; copies of **Describe.doc** and **Ordering.doc** from the CD; photocopies of **Describe.doc**, **Ordering.doc** and **Sorted.doc**; a selection of objects that have three or more of the properties listed on **Describe.doc**; PE hoops or sorting rings, glue, writing and drawing materials and scissors.

Activity A

What to do

With the whole class, choose an object at random from your selection, and open a blank copy of **Objects.doc** on the computer screen. (Make sure you can see both pages of the activity on the screen at once: click *View > Page Layout* then set the 'Zoom' to 'Two Pages'.) Look at the words on the left-hand side of the computer screen, and read the two words in the top box: 'Big', 'Small' – which word best describes the object you have chosen? Recap how to select the word they want by clicking on it with the left mouse button, and how to move it by moving the cursor to the edge until it changes to a cross. Move the word from the left side of the screen to the same-coloured box on the right. Repeat this for the words in the blue and green boxes.

Each box on the right side of the screen should now contain one word that describes the object in your hand.

At the computer

In small groups or individually, ask children to choose an item from the selection (such as a small, blue piece of paper). They can then take this to the computer and, using their own copy of **Objects.doc**, choose the words from the left-hand side of the screen that best describe their object. Once they have chosen each word, they should 'click and drag' it to the right-hand side of the screen to create a description of their object. When complete, save the work to the children's individual folders, or print it out and display the descriptions.

When printing out work from either Activity A or B, remember that you only need to print out page 2 of the file, as page 1 will either be blank, or of no use for assessment purposes. To print only page 2 of the document, select the 'Page range' option in the Print dialogue box, and set it to page 2 only before clicking 'OK'. This can cut your paper usage in half!

Set the 'Page Range' so that it only prints the pages you need, thus saving paper.

At their desks

If there is not enough time for all children to attempt this activity at the computer, ask them to use a photocopy of both pages of **Objects.doc** and complete the activity by choosing and cutting out the words they need to describe their object. They can either stick the words from page 1 straight onto the object or they can stick them into the label frames on page 2. These could then be displayed as a set of words or cut out to go on display with the objects.

Activity B

What to do

This activity also asks children to create labels to describe objects that will allow them to sort things into groups. Show the children a blank copy of **Describe.doc** on the computer screen, and explain that they need to select three words as they did before, but that the words and objects are different.

Read the list to the whole class and explain that these words describe the texture of the materials. Once they have decided on the words that best describe their object, they should 'click and drag' them from the left-hand page to the spaces on the right.

At the computer

It would be a good idea to start this activity with any children who did not take part in the 'At the computer' work from Activity A. Allow individuals or small groups to choose an object from the new selection, and to choose words from a blank copy of **Describe.doc** to complete the task.

At their desks

When the describing labels have been printed out ask the children, working in the same groups as they did at the computer, to cut the labels out and put one word into each of three PE hoops on the floor. They should then choose items from the selection and put them into the hoop that matches the description (for example, grouping all the smooth items, all the rough items and all the hard items).

Once they have grouped three types of object they can either record their findings on a photocopy of **Sorted.doc**, sticking the printed labels in the spaces next to each of the hoops, or you could take a photograph of the sorting hoops to keep for your records. If there is not enough time for all children to complete the 'At the computer' part of the activity, they can still label the sorting hoops with a photocopy of the key words from **Objects.doc**.

The sorting work could be presented as a 'Hands-on' sorting display. Place three hoops on a display table with labelled descriptions in each hoop and a selection of suitable items for the children to sort. Try changing the labels every week so the children don't get bored with the display.

Conclusion

Revise the skills needed to 'click and drag' an object across the screen. Ask individual children to demonstrate good practice to the rest of the class. Also ask the children to describe in their own words how to 'click and drag' an object. Can they think of anything else that could be moved across the screen (for example, a picture or icon)?

Adapting the idea

❏ Display the work from both activities alongside each other. Try displaying an object on the wall, surrounded by the describing labels made by the children. Attach three long pieces of string next to the object and let the children move the string and stick it next to the words that describe it.

❏ Why not play games with the children when they have created their labels? Put the group of objects in a pile on the floor and ask the children to sit in a circle around them. The children can then take it in turns to read out the words they have chosen to describe their object, while the other children guess which item they have chosen.

❏ Use a copy of **Ordering.doc** (either printed out or on-screen) to sort three of the items from the main activities into order, for example small, smaller, smallest.

A label for everything

Introduction

Look around the classroom with the children and identify objects in the room that they know the name of. Explain that they are going to choose things to add labels to so that when other children come into the classroom they know what things are.

There are four such labelling activities on the CD for this project that cover a wide range of topics. They will allow children to label classroom items (**Classroom.doc**), parts of the body (**Body.doc**), parts of a computer (**Computer.doc**) and fiction and non-fiction books (**Books.doc**).

Each of these four activities has been created using the same basic format, but changes have been made to the shape of the boxes to add variety. Different groups could work on different files to allow differentiated vocabulary work.

ICT objectives

❏ To understand that objects can be labelled for identification.
❏ To revise the 'click and drag' skills needed to move text.

Resources

You will need: access to *Microsoft Word*; copies of **Classroom.doc**, **Body.doc**, **Computer.doc** and **Books.doc** from the CD; photocopies of each of the four files from the CD; classroom objects: a large doll or picture of the human body, a computer and books for labelling; writing and drawing materials, scissors, Blu-Tack, sticky-backed plastic or laminating pouches.

At the computer

Open up one of the four files as a demonstration for the whole class. (Make sure you can see the whole activity: click *View > Page Layout* then set 'Zoom' to 'Two Pages'.) Recap 'clicking and dragging' words from the left-hand page to the right-hand page, and ask the children to choose objects from the list of words on the left to create labels to add to the objects they are working on.

Working individually or in groups, ask them to create two or three labels in the blank spaces on the right of the screen. When they have done this, save the file to the children's individual folder and print the labels out.

The four different files can be used for children of different abilities. **Classroom.doc** is suitable for less confident children, **Computer.doc** for more confident children. When completing **Book.doc** children need to choose a favourite book, then decide if it is fiction or non-fiction and drag the word across. They can then choose if they want to label the author, illustrator or title of the book.

At their desks

Once the pages have been printed, ask the children to cut the shapes out to create their labels. They could design and colour borders before sticking the labels to the objects they have selected. **Computer.doc** has been created using 'outline letters', so children can colour their own letters before sticking them on the computer, and **Books.doc** allows space for the children to write the title, author's or illustrator's name.

By using a blank printout of any of the files, children can complete these activities by hand, cutting the words out and sticking them into the border boxes. More confident children could write the words in the spaces themselves, using the list as a guide.

Conclusion

Look around the classroom and ask the children to find as many labelled objects as they can. Can they think of any objects they see at home or on their way to school that are labelled or communicate information about what they are? Remind the children that words and simple pictures are a great way to pass on information.

Adapting the idea

❏ Labels can be created for just about anything! Why not try using the AutoShapes feature (located on the 'Drawing' toolbar, which can be found by clicking *View > Toolbars > Drawing*) to create borders for labelling activities covering the weather, days of the week, seasons, names to go on the 'Learning Support Assistant' board, group name labels, or for identifying different types of materials in science (such as plastic or wood) or punctuation marks in a story.

❏ All of these activities could be adapted so that the children can play 'Guess what or who I am' games (see 'Adapting the idea' for the 'Describe me' activities above)

Butterfly

Introduction

In this activity, children can label parts of a butterfly by moving text around the screen. They will need to be familiar with the basic parts of a butterfly's body, but only simple parts have been chosen to allow children to concentrate on the skills required.

This activity is ideal to be taught alongside any literacy or science work within the curriculum that involves labelling a diagram. It would be useful to remind the children that pictures can have labels to give us more information about them, just as objects can.

ICT objectives

❏ To understand that parts of an object can be labelled for identification.

❏ To revise the 'click and drag' skills needed to move text.

Resources

You will need: access to *Microsoft Word*; copies of **Butterfly.doc** from the CD; photocopies of CD-ROM activity **Butterfly.doc** and an enlarged A3 copy of **Butterfly.doc**; a whiteboard, writing and drawing materials, scissors, glue, black paper, brightly coloured tissue paper and Blu-Tack.

What to do

Draw a picture of a bird on the board and brainstorm one-word descriptions of the picture, concentrating on the parts of the body the children can see, such as wings, head, legs.

Write the words on the board on top of the picture and in the same colour; encourage the children to notice that as you write they can't see either the picture or the words clearly! Show that if you write the words around the outside of the picture and put a line pointing to the relevant part they will be able to see both the words and picture at the same time: this is another way of labelling. Continue this activity with a variety of pictures encouraging the children to label the objects.

Open a copy of **Butterfly.doc** on-screen. Show the children the picture of the butterfly and together read the words on the right-hand side of the screen. Choose children to come and point to the line they think will join up to each of the words in turn. This will help reinforce the names of the sections of the butterfly's body.

Now revise with the children how to 'click and drag' an object across the screen: they should click on a word and, when the squares appear, should 'click and drag' the word across the screen, dropping it next to the label line.

At the computer

In pairs or individually, ask children to work on their own copy of **Butterfly.doc**, moving the words to match up with the label lines. When they have completed the activity, their work can be saved to their individual folders for assessment and printing out.

At their desks

If time is limited and not all children can complete the activity at the computer, hand out printed copies of **Butterfly.doc** and ask children to cut the labels out from the sheet and stick them in their correct place. More confident children could write the words next to the label lines, copying from the labels.

Simple words have been chosen for the parts of the butterfly on the CD, but more complicated words could be added, such as antenna, thorax or abdomen, if children are familiar with them.

If extra support is needed for some children, the colour of the lines can be changed to help them match the words, for example blue text box matches up with a blue line.

Conclusion

Revise the skills needed to 'click and drag' an object across the screen. Ask individual children to demonstrate good practice to the rest of the class. Also ask the children to describe in their own words how to 'click and drag' an object. Always try and choose different children each time so that every child has the opportunity to demonstrate their newly found skills!

Adapting the idea

❏ Children could paint their own pictures of butterflies, or create a stained-glass butterfly using black paper and tissue paper: cut out a butterfly shape from black paper and cut several shapes 2–3cm wide from the wings. Stick pieces of tissue paper over the shapes to create the patterns on the wings. These butterflies look very effective stuck on a window with the light shining through the tissue paper, and children can then cut out the labels from the activity sheet and stick them next to the appropriate butterfly parts on the window.

❑ Depending on your topic work, why not change the Clip Art so the children can label pictures of dogs, cats, people or cars?

❑ Try changing the words on the right-hand side of the page into adjectives such as *red*, *shiny* or *long* for other Literacy Hour work.

Workshop

How to create your own name labels

Creating the name labels activity relies on similar principles to the word bank activities in Chapter 3 – they are both essentially empty boxes and text frames arranged on the page that can be filled with the children's work. Because the activities for this chapter use *Microsoft Word* rather than *Microsoft Publisher*, some of the techniques for creating the files are slightly different.

Resources

You will need: access to *Microsoft Word*.

What to do

Open *Microsoft Word* and start a new document. At the moment you have a blank page but you can't see the whole page. You will need to set the view to 'Page Layout', and make sure you can see the whole page on the screen at once. To do this, click *View > Page Layout*, then set 'Zoom' to 'Whole Page'. You will now be able to see the whole page on your screen. It is important that the whole page is visible in these activities so the children do not have to scroll up and down the page. If you have any problems seeing the whole activity on the screen at any time, check the 'Readme' file on the CD that accompanies this book for some possible solutions.

Now you will need to make a text box using the text box from the 'Drawing' toolbar. (To display this toolbar if it's not there already,

These three buttons allow you to change the colour of the background, line and text respectively.

This button will allow you to change the thickness of the border line.

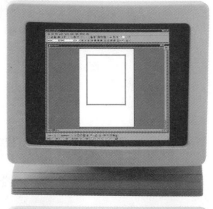

click *View > Toolbars* and choose 'Drawing'.) Draw a box by positioning the cursor at the top-left of where you want the box to appear, then 'clicking and dragging' with the mouse to create the box. Choose the colour and thickness of the box's border by clicking on the icons on the 'Drawing' toolbar.

Even though there is no text in your box yet, you can still change the style of what will be typed in there later. Make sure you have a flashing cursor inside the box, then choose a font, style, size and colour from the option boxes. The text in **Name.doc** on the CD is 120pt Arial bold, but you could use any font or size you wish. It is also a good idea to set the text in the centre of the box so that it appears in the middle of the label rather than at either side.

Finally, repeat this process to create three (or more) text boxes on one page, then save the finished template to your teacher's file.

How to create your own describing and labelling projects

This workshop covers how to make files based on the 'Describe me' and 'A label for everything' activities, which both rely on similar layouts and which are easy to create in *Microsoft Word*.

Resources

You will need: access to *Microsoft Word*.

What to do

Open *Microsoft Word* and create a new document. The first thing that you need to do when creating an activity similar to **Objects.doc** or **Describing.doc** is to be able to see two pages side by side. To do this you should add a second page to the document, by clicking *Insert >*

Break, and selecting 'Page Break', then clicking 'OK': this inserts a second page into your document. To view these two pages side by side, click *View > Page Layout*, then set 'Zoom' to 'Two pages'. You should end up with a screen that looks like the one on the right.

To recreate the CD activity **Object.doc**, start by creating six text boxes – three on each page. Using the text box tool from the bottom toolbar, 'click and drag' the pointer to create a box roughly one-third the size of the page. Choose a different colour for the line around the top, middle and bottom boxes on each page from the palette. These boxes form your background.

As with the word bank activities in Chapter 3, each piece of text that can be moved on the page needs to be in its own text box. Use the text box tool to draw smaller text boxes for each word (these don't need a border), and change the font, style, size and colour appropriate to the words – for example big or small text, or different colours to represent different names of colours.

Repeat this for each set of words, placing them inside the boxes on

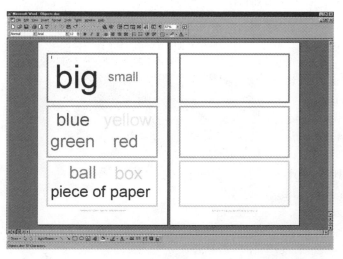

the left-hand page so that they can be moved across to the other page by the children. If any of your words disappear at any point, they haven't gone forever – it's just that they have disappeared behind the boxes you created earlier. To change this, select the box behind which your text has vanished, then click *Draw > Order > Send behind text* and your text should reappear.

To add a variety to the pages rather than simple boxes, why not use AutoShapes which relate to the topic you are looking at? These can be found by clicking *Draw > AutoShapes*, and are created just as you would an ordinary text box.

Fonts and colours can also be used to create lively effects: to create the outlined letters used in **Computer.doc**, for example, create a normal text box and type in the required word. Then click *Format > Font* and a box of options will appear; select 'Outline' from the 'Effects' box and click 'OK' to apply the effect. Take time to experiment and you can create striking effects easily.

When you are happy with the way your file appears, save the template to your teacher's folder.

How to create your own butterfly activity

Resources

You will need: access to *Microsoft Word*; suitable Clip Art for the activity (the butterfly image used in **Butterfly.doc** can be found in the 'Workshop components' subfolder on the CD).

What to do

Open *Microsoft Word* and create a new document. The page will automatically be created in the portrait position, so to change it to landscape click *File > Page Setup*, then select 'Landscape' from the 'Paper Size' tab and click 'OK'. Set the view to 'Page Layout' and the 'Zoom' to 'Whole Page' as before so that the children can work on a whole page at once.

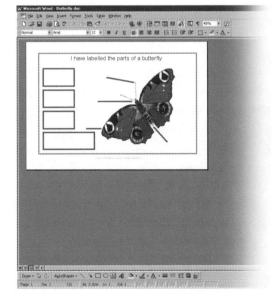

To create the four labels on the left-hand side of the page, use the text box tool to draw four boxes, then style the line and text inside them as you wish using the fill and colour options on the 'Drawing' toolbar, adding words appropriate to the level of knowledge of your class and the subject matter you will be labelling.

Before you insert the Clip Art for the children to label, it is a good idea to create a text box that is sized, shaped and positioned where you want the picture to be; the image will then automatically be inserted to fill this box at the correct size.

Draw the text box as you did for the labels (but this box won't need a line around it) then, with the

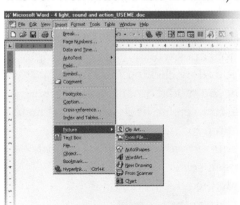

text box selected (squares will be around the edge) select *Insert > Picture*, and click on either 'Clip Art' or 'From File', depending on where your picture is stored (if you know where the image is kept, choose 'From File'; if you wish to browse a gallery of possible images, choose 'Clip Art').

Locate your picture from the dialogue box that

appears, then click on 'Insert' to add the picture to the page – it should appear in the correct position and at the correct size. If you need to alter the position of the picture, move the cursor to a corner of the box until it changes to an arrowed cross: ↖. 'Click and drag' the picture to size.

If you want to point more precisely to parts of the picture, use the 'Arrow' tool immediately next to the 'Line' tool (circled).

The labelling lines were created with the 'Line' tool from the bottom 'Drawing' toolbar (see above). Drawing a line uses the same technique as drawing a text box: select the tool then 'click and drag' on the screen from where you want the line to start and end in order to create the line of the desired length. Change the colour of the line by using the arrow next to the 'Line Colour' then select a colour.

To change the thickness of the line select the 'Line Style' icon and select the width you require (see below).

When drawing the label lines on the screen, choose a thicker line so that the children can see what the line is pointing to more easily.

Finish the page off with two more boxes: a title and a border around the page. These are both text boxes; draw them on the page and style them as you wish. When you draw the border around the whole page, all your other work may disappear – this means that the box is on top of the rest of the work and is hiding it. To fix this, right-click on the frame that is covering the rest of the page, then click *Order > Send Behind Text* and the rest of the work should reappear.

Save the finished work to your teacher's file and it is ready for the children to use in lessons to practise their labelling and 'clicking and dragging' skills.

6 : Follow me!

Vocabulary and definitions

Control: to tell an object or person what to do.

Instruction: a statement that gives an object a specific command to do something.

Order: to put instructions one after another so that they can be followed step by step to produce a result.

Sequence: a set of instructions in an order that will produce the desired effect.

Turn off: to deactivate a device.

Turn on: to activate a device.

Project overview

Understanding instructions

Project	Subject link	ICT objective
On and off	ICT	To know that equipment needs to be controlled
On tape	ICT	To control an object through a series of instructions
Follow the leader	ICT	To use a common language to deliver instructions

CD resources

These activities are in the 'Follow me' folder on the CD that accompanies this book. They will open with any version of *Microsoft Publisher* from *Publisher 98* onwards. Please note that when you first open these files on a computer, you may get a message telling you that the default printer cannot be found. This is normal, and should be ignored. See the CD's 'Readme' file for more information.

The files you will need are: **Blank maze.pub**, **Cards.pub**, **Finding.pub**, **House.pub**, **Maze.pub**, **Sequencing.pub** (which contains three differentiated activities in one file) and **Tape recorder.pub** (which contains three differentiated activities in one file).

Taking control

In this chapter children will have the opportunity to discover that some objects need to be controlled to make them work. Tape recorders, TVs, cars and many other objects all need us to tell them what to do before they will do what they are intended to. Some objects just need to be turned on and off, for example a tap, radio or TV, and others need a set of sequenced instructions to make them work, for example a tape recorder, computer or car.

When the children start to think about the world around them, in their homes and at school, they will discover that there are a great number of objects that need to be controlled. They will have the opportunity to investigate how different things are controlled by pressing buttons, flicking switches or simply by turning them on or off.

They will also need to understand that when they give a series of instructions it is important that these are put in an accurate order. For example, when making a cake the ingredients need to be added in a certain order, mixed and then cooked – there is no point in cooking it if the mixing hasn't taken place!

Instructions can be given in many different ways, but the children will look mainly at those that are written and spoken in this chapter. They will have the opportunity to control both objects and other children, giving a series of instructions in order to complete a series of tasks.

Projects

☐ On and off

Introduction

Discuss with the whole class different kinds of technology they see being used around them every day, for example the television, cooker, computer or lights. Talk about how these items work: do they work all the time or do you have to turn them on and off? Use the television as an example: it needs to be switched on and off, it doesn't stay on all the time. We can control when we want to watch it.

If you can, show the children a remote control that operates something, such as a toy car, for example, so they can look at the way it is controlled. They will usually find that there is a switch on the car that needs to be turned on before they press the buttons or turn the switches to make it move – it will certainly get all the children interested! Try asking them how they think a remote control actually 'works'.

ICT objective

❏ To understand that some equipment and machines need to be controlled.

Resources

You will need: access to *Microsoft Publisher*; photocopies of **House.pub** from the CD (print one copy and then photocopy enough for the whole class); household magazines or catalogues to cut up, glue, scissors, writing and drawing materials, cardboard, string, coathangers, sorting rings, a selection of toys that need to be turned on before they will work (such as a pull-back car) and a remote-control car.

What to do

Encourage the children to think about other things we need to turn on to make them work, either by pressing a button, flicking a switch or by twisting a dial. Write a class list of 'Turn on-able' items, grouping them into three categories on the board:

Pressing buttons	Flicking switches	Turning
TV	Lights	Cooker
Video	Plug sockets	Old watches
Doorbell		Wind-up toys
		Taps

Talk about where in the house the items written on the board might be found: the cooker in the kitchen, the TV in the living room, taps in the bathroom and toys in the bedroom. Encourage the children to think about all the things they use at home that they have to control or turn on before they will work.

Encourage the children to think of everyday objects that they need to control.

At their desks

Give each child a copy of **House.pub**, and ask the children to look through magazines and catalogues to find as many items as they can that need to be turned on to work. They should then cut the pictures out and stick them in the appropriate room on their copy of **House.pub**, for example a microwave in the kitchen or a TV in the living room.

Conclusion

Ask children to share their findings with the rest of the class and demonstrate how they turn these objects on (do they press, push or turn them, for example?). The children can add their findings to the class list created at the start of the lesson. Encourage the children to think of more items around the house, school or outside that can be controlled.

Adapting the idea

The items that the children find in the catalogues could be used as backing paper for a display of work about this topic.

The children could mount some of their pictures onto card and make 'Turn on and off' mobiles by hanging the pictures from coathangers.

Try giving the children a selection of toys that need to be controlled before they will work: toy cars that need to be pushed, remote-control toys, wind-up and spinning toys are all useful to use. Encourage the children to investigate the items and discover for themselves how to make them work.

Set up three sorting hoops as part of a display so the children can sort items into groups according to how they are controlled, for example pushing buttons, turning dials and flicking switches.

Look at any programmable toys you have in school. 'Roamers' or 'Pixies' are toys that need to be controlled, and are great for experimenting with!

On tape

Introduction

Most children are familiar with the way a tape recorder works, but don't take this for granted. Show the children that a tape recorder will not play or record sounds without being controlled, or told what to do. Explain that to turn the tape recorder on we have to press buttons, and which buttons we press will determine what the tape recorder will do. For example if we want to play some music we must tell the machine what to do by pressing the 'Play' button. The tape recorder will continue to play until we tell it to stop by pressing the 'Stop' button. If we press the 'Record' button the machine will record all the sounds around it until we tell it to stop, again by selecting the 'Stop' button.

ICT objective

❏ To understand that machines and technological objects can be controlled by giving them a series of instructions that will cause them to do what we want.

Resources

You will need: access to *Microsoft Publisher*; printed copies of **Tape recorder.pub** and **Sequencing.pub** (which has three differentiated sequencing activities) from the CD; a tape recorder with a tape.

What to do

Show the class a set of four cards from **Tape recorder.pub** (you could laminate the cards to protect them). The four simple cards show the commands a tape recorder needs to be able to play a piece of music. The cards demonstrate a simple 'playing music' sequence: a tape in the recorder but nothing is happening (first command); the 'Play' button being pressed and music being played (second); the 'Stop' button being pressed with the music no longer playing (third); and the 'Eject' button being pressed and the tape being removed (fourth).

Invite a child to come and order the cards to show the correct sequence needed to play the music and remove the tape. Ask the rest of the class if they agree on the order.

At the computer

Once the children have agreed on what they think to be the correct sequence, they can try it out for real by following the cards to make a real tape recorder work. If they have got the sequence correct music will play and they will be able to remove the tape from the recorder. Ask children in small groups to try and complete this task with a real tape recorder, following the sequence cards.

Try giving a group the instructions in the wrong order: what will happen? Explain to them that if the instructions are in the wrong order the machine won't work, it can only do what you tell it to do when you press the buttons. Point out that the machine cannot think for itself like we can, so it needs us to tell it what to do.

At their desks

The file **Sequencing.pub** on the CD contains three differentiated worksheets in one file, asking children to order four, six and eight pictures based on making a tape recorder play music. Print out and photocopy as many copies of each sheet as required.

Working independently, the children can cut out the pictures of the tape recorder and stick them on to a plain piece of paper in the correct order. When they have completed this task they could use a real tape recorder to check that their sequencing is correct.

Conclusion

Discuss with the children any objects that they might have at home that they can control. You may find that they will have thought of more ideas than those put forward at the start of the lesson because they have had time to think about it. Reinforce the idea that there are many different types of machine that can be controlled once they have been given a set of instructions.

Adapting the idea

❑ Give children blank pictures of a tape recorder (or you could try photocopying a real tape recorder), so that they can try creating their own sequencing pictures; encourage them to include the 'Fast forward' and 'Rewind' buttons.

❑ Allow a group of children to use a real tape recorder and ask them to write a set of instructions for another group of children to follow.

❑ There are lots of different activities that can be sequenced, for example making a cake, driving a car or building a model. The children could try sequencing these activities, then look at the importance of following the correct order of the instructions. What would happen if they beat an egg before they cracked it open? Or they tried to put the key in the ignition before they opened the car door?

Follow the leader

Introduction

During the next set of activities, children will become aware that people can also be controlled by giving them a set of clear and accurate instructions. The best place to introduce this discussion about direction and movement is during a PE lesson.

Start by revising right and left turns – you need to be confident that children will turn the right way when given instructions! Try playing 'Simon says' type games using instructions such as 'Simon says… wave your right hand', '…hop on your left leg', '…wiggle your fingers on your left hand' or '…put your right hand on your left leg'.

If children still find this identification difficult, try sticking coloured arrow stickers on the back of their hands (to coincide with later activities it would be a good idea to colour-code right as green and left as orange) as a reminder.

Tell the children that they are robots and you are going to give them instructions about how to move. Ask them to stand in rows of ten, one behind another, and give them an instruction such as 'Walk forward'. All the children will walk at different paces, some will take one step and others will keep walking – this is not a good instruction! Highlight that when giving instructions it is important to say, for example, exactly how far to walk forward. Encourage the children to choose 'one step' as the distance for each instruction (so 'Walk forward' means 'Take one step forward').

Now you can play lots of class games using just the instructions 'Walk forwards' and 'Walk backwards'. Try giving instructions one at a time, or a whole series: forwards, forwards, forwards, backwards, backwards, forwards. (Check that all children are taking roughly the same size steps.)

Next you can introduce turning instructions: 'Turn left' and 'Turn right'. Encourage the children to decide that this means a 90 degree turn, on the spot, in either direction. (Try using the coloured arrow stickers again for the children who are still having difficulties.) Highlight that if they turn four times in the same direction they will end up facing the same direction as they started!

When the children are comfortable with this, try mixing both sets of instructions: forwards, turn right, forwards, backwards, turn left. Keep checking that all children are facing the same way when they finish! They are bound to find this quite difficult at first, but the more they practise the easier it will become!

Let children work in pairs giving each other instructions to move around a simple obstacle course – this will give them valuable practice in creating and following sequences of instructions, and will provide a better context for the rest of the work in this activity.

ICT objectives

❏ To understand that instructions can be given using common languages or symbols.
❏ To use instructions to 'control' another person's movements.
❏ To predict where a series of instructions will lead.

Resources

You will need: access to *Microsoft Publisher*; copies of **Maze.pub** from the CD (which contains three differentiated activities) and **Blank maze.pub**; printed copies of **Cards.pub** (one set of four cards per pair of children) and **Finding.pub** from the CD; card, Blu-Tack, sticky-backed plastic or laminating pouches, scissors, stickers, writing and drawing materials.

What to do

Before the lesson, print out enough sets of directional cards from **Cards.pub** for the children to use in the lesson (if the printouts are in colour, it will help less confident children recognise the difference between the directions). These cards could be laminated for future use and durability.

For the second part of this activity the children will need copies of **Maze.pub**. There are three differentiated activities on this file to suit children with different abilities: page 1 is the simplest maze, page 3 the most complex.

Gather the whole class together, and show them a set of arrow cards from **Cards.pub**. Explain that they can use these to guide people from one place to another, as they did in the earlier PE lesson. Explain that each arrow tells them which way to walk, and remind them that each card represents one step in the direction of the arrow.

Pick two points in the classroom to navigate between, labelling them A and B. Ask for two volunteers to try and complete a sequence of instructions to move successfully from point A to point B using only the instructions on the cards. One child should use the cards to create a sequence, and the other child should follow their instructions. Ask the navigator to stick their sequence up on the board as they create their sequence. Once they have finished, ask the class if they agree with the sequence.

At their desks

Give pairs or small groups of children their own set of direction cards, and ask them to try and create a set of instructions to navigate between different points of the classroom by sequencing the cards on their desks. (To avoid too much moving around, you may want to ask the groups to try and work the routes out in their heads first.) Explain that it is easier to start with a short route, and to gradually increase the number of instructions as they become more confident.

When the children think they have a complete set of instructions, ask them to record the sequence, using a copy of **Finding.pub** to draw their start and finish points, and recording the sequence of instructions in the spaces along the bottom of the page. You could then ask groups to swap sets of instructions to see if they actually work when followed.

It is a good idea to let the children predict where a set of instructions will lead them before they try them out. When swapping instructions in their groups they can create a set of instructions from their chosen starting point, but not say where their instructions are leading! The other group must predict where they will end up before following the instructions.

Conclusion

Highlight that instructions will change depending upon the starting point. Where the children start from or the direction they are facing will change the directions. For example, a set of instructions on how to get to the teacher's desk will be different depending on whether you start from the door or the window. Try and encourage the children to discover this for themselves by letting them choose their own starting point but all working towards the same finishing point – when they compare their results they will all be different but they will all be correct!

Adapting the idea

❑ Set a treasure trail by completing a copy of **Finding.pub** yourself for the children to follow. Ask them to predict where they think the instructions will lead them, and to draw where they think they will end up in the space on the sheet before following the instructions to see if they were right.

❑ You can print a blank copy of a maze (**Blank maze.pub**) and create your own by colouring in as many squares as you need. When you colour the squares in think about a pattern so the children have to weave their way through the maze using all the arrows.

❑ Why not try giving children an ordered set of the arrow cards and ask them to draw the sequence of arrows onto the maze grid.

❑ Try playing the 'Simon says' game at the start of PE lessons as a warm-up activity!

Workshop

How to make your own mazes

These maze activities are easy to make yourself with a copy of *Microsoft Publisher*. Of course, if you wish to print out a copy of **Blank maze.pub** and colour squares to create the maze you can do so, but this workshop will show how to create a maze from scratch with your own Clip Art images.

Resources

You will need: access to *Microsoft Publisher*; suitable Clip Art images.

What to do

Open *Publisher* and create a new, blank document. You may need to set the page so that it appears as landscape rather than portrait. To do this, click *Edit > Page Setup* and select 'Landscape' in the 'Choose an orientation' box at the bottom. Then click 'OK' to change the setup of the page.

The basis of the maze is a table, into which you can place Clip Art images or obstacles for the children to navigate around. To draw a table, select the table tool from the top toolbar, then place the pointer at one corner of where you want the table to appear and click the left mouse button. Holding the mouse button down, drag the pointer until it creates a table the size you want, then release the mouse button; a 'Create Table' dialogue box will appear. Here you can specify the number of rows and columns in your table. This can change depending on the ability of your children, but 7 columns and 5 rows is a good starting point. Select [None] as the table format, as this table only needs to be a series of boxes at the moment. Click 'OK' to create the table on the page.

At the moment the table is only a box, and there are no lines to divide up the individual cells (the grey lines you can see on-screen won't print out), so you need to add a grid to all the cells. You will need to apply this to the whole table, so will need to select all the cells before changing the style. Click anywhere in the table with the left mouse button – this will highlight the table, and two grey bars will appear at the top and left of the table. Click once in the very top left-hand corner of these grey bars to select the whole table (it should turn black). Click the 'Line/Border Style' button (below). Select 'More styles', then in the dialogue box that appears (as shown on the left), choose 'Grid' from the 'Preset' box and click 'OK'. The table should change to a proper grid, with each of the cells divided up by solid lines that will appear when the file is printed out, as well as on screen.

Creating the maze is simply a matter of filling certain squares of the table with colour to create obstacles. Click with the left mouse button in any cell of the table in which you want to create an obstacle, then click the 'Fill' button and choose a colour from the menu that appears. Repeat this for each square you want to turn into an obstacle.

The arrows at the bottom of the page are created using the 'AutoShapes' tool on the 'Drawing' toolbar – click *Draw > AutoShapes* and choose 'Block arrows', then draw the shapes in position at the bottom of the page, using the 'Fill' tool to change their colour.

Lastly, insert Clip Art images if you wish at the start and end of the route through the maze (click *Insert > Picture > From File* to add Clip Art), and add a text box for the instructions. Save the file to your folder, and print it out ready for use.

Clicking the 'Line and Border Style' button (circled above) brings up the 'Border Style' dialogue box.

7: Looking at text

Vocabulary and definitions

BACKSPACE key: when pressed, will delete the letter immediately to the left of the cursor.

DELETE key: used to delete the character immediately to the right of the cursor.

ENTER/RETURN key: key on the keyboard used to create a new line.

SHIFT key: used to create a capital letter when pressed in conjunction with a letter key.

SPACE bar: the key used to create a blank space between words.

Text: written language.

Project overview

Writing stories

Project	Subject link	ICT objective
Spaced out	Literacy	To enter and format text on computer
Enter here	Literacy	To format and space out text
And, and, and!	Literacy	To edit and improve text on-screen

CD resources

The files for this chapter are kept in the 'Looking at text' folder on the CD that accompanies this book. The files will open in *Microsoft WordPad*, although they will also work in *Microsoft Word*, and to work correctly, **Bubbles 1.doc** to **Bubbles 4.doc** can only be opened in *Microsoft Word*. They are designed to be compatible with all versions of *WordPad* (which comes as standard with *Windows* and can be found by clicking *Start > Programs > Accessories > WordPad*), and versions of *Word* newer than *Word 97*.

The files you will need are **Bubbles 1.doc** to **Bubbles 4.doc**, **Seaside.doc** and **Shadow.doc**.

The Clip Art used in the speech bubbles activities is stored in the 'Workshop components' subfolder, and can be used to create your own speech bubbles activities.

The text for these activities is taken from the *Project Gutenberg* website (www.promo.net/pg), which carries a vast number of 'etexts' on its site that are freely downloadable for use, and can be used by pupils and teachers as a valuable resource.

Writing stories

In this chapter children will use a simple word-processing package to manipulate and create pieces of text. *Microsoft WordPad* is a basic word-processing package that allows children the freedom to create and edit text in a less-complicated environment than *Microsoft Word*. Any work created in *WordPad* can also be opened in *Microsoft Word* so all files can be easily transferred.

During the following activities the children will compare hand-written and typed work, and will become familiar with a number of special keys on the keyboard and their functions. They will learn about the RETURN key and when it is used, using the DELETE and BACKSPACE keys to remove unwanted text, and become familiar with the . (full stop), SHIFT key, and the SPACE bar. They will also have the opportunity to manipulate the size, colour and font of their work by using the three specific formatting tools (see 'Skills practice', below).

Skills practice

For the activities in this chapter the children will need to become familiar with basic skills needed to word process a piece of work. Some of these skills were introduced in Chapter 3. Give children the freedom to develop these skills by allowing them to type words and sentences into *WordPad* just as you would let them practise handwriting. It is a good idea to stick coloured stickers on specific regularly used keys (SHIFT, BACKSPACE, SPACE bar, for example) to help the children recognise them with the minimum of support.

The children will need to become familiar with three basic functions:

❏ To change the font (sometimes known as typeface), children need to click the down arrow next to the name of the font in the top toolbar and choose from the selection of different fonts that appears. This will obviously depend on the fonts you have installed on your computer, and may appear slightly different depending on whether you use *WordPad* or *Word*; *WordPad* may not display the fonts themselves, only their names.

❏ To change the size of the text, children should use the font size box, either clicking inside the box and typing a number, or clicking on the down arrow and choosing a number

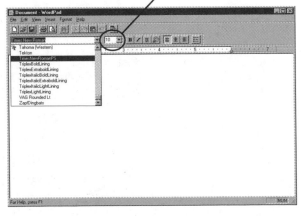

Choose your type size from the drop down menu.

from the list. The size of text is measured in points (pts) – there are 72 of these to the inch, or 28 to the centimetre. Thus, 72 pt text is approximately an inch tall, and 8 pt text is quite small. (The type you are reading now is 10.5 pt.)

❑ To change the colour of the text, use the button on the drawing toolbar, and pick a colour from the palette that appears (see below).

It is worth noting that making changes to text already typed on the screen requires the children to select the text they wish to change so that it is 'highlighted' before they make the changes. This requires children to use the mouse to select words by placing the pointer at the start of the word(s) they wish to highlight, then clicking the left mouse button and dragging the pointer until the word is selected (it will turn to a black background). Any changes to the font, size or colour will now apply only to the word(s) that have been highlighted

There are lots of simple activities children can do to practise using these tools and their typing skills before or as they are completing the projects in this chapter. Printouts of the activities can be used to create an eye-catching display. Why not ask the children to:

❑ Write their name ten times, each time growing or shrinking in size.
❑ Write their name in ten different fonts.
❑ Write their name in ten different colours.
❑ Write simple sentences using a combination of fonts, sizes and colours.
❑ Create a number line 1–10 (or 20), choosing a different colour for odd and even numbers.

Projects

Spaced out

Introduction

Start this activity by showing the children a piece of typed text (ideally try and get hold of a story written by an older child in your school to look at anonymously). Discuss how neat the work looks, that you can't see any mistakes, you can't even tell who wrote it by looking at the handwriting! Now look at a handwritten story (try to get – or create – a rather scruffy piece with lots of mistakes and crossings out). Encourage the children to compare the two pieces of writing. Ask the children why they think books are typed and not written by hand. Look at a few different pieces of text: poems, stories or newspapers, and discuss the different styles and shape of the words.

Choose a book and read the children a few sentences from it, but read it without the spaces! Highlight how important it is to put spaces between words, without them the writing doesn't make sense because all the words become one!

Show the children where the SPACE bar is on the keyboard. Choose a coloured sticker and stick it on the key so that the children can find it quickly when they are working. Point out that the SPACE bar is the longest key on the keyboard, so there are no excuses for missing them out!

ICT objectives

❏ To recognise the differences between written and typed text.
❏ To know that text can be entered and corrected using a computer.
❏ To know that it is important to put spaces between words.
❏ To recognise that the SHIFT key is used to create a capital letter.

Resources

You will need: access to *Microsoft Word*; copies of **Bubbles 1.doc** to **Bubbles 4.doc** from the CD; printed copies of **Bubbles 1.doc** to **Bubbles 4.doc**; writing and drawing materials, glue and scissors.

The children can create conversations between the characters on the worksheets in the speech bubbles (like this).

What to do

Create a new, blank document in *Microsoft Word*, and type in a simple sentence (perhaps choose one from your current Big Book or reading scheme), leaving the spaces between the words out. Make sure the text is in a large font size (36 pt or greater) so that all the children can see the words on the screen, and because children often find it difficult to place the cursor accurately when the writing is small.

Ask the children what is wrong with what you have typed on the screen. Explain that they need to use the mouse to move the pointer, the I, to where a space is needed. Demonstrate this: when the cursor is in the right place carefully click the left mouse button. A black '|' will flash in the space. Press the SPACE bar to put a gap between the words, highlighting that only one space is needed between each word.

Allow volunteers to come to the front to add spaces between the rest of the words on the screen. Remind the children not to panic if they make a mistake, recap with them that they can use the BACKSPACE key to undo the error!

At the computer

Ask children, individually, to write their own sentences using a new, blank document. They could either write their own sentence, or could copy the one used in the demonstration. Remind them how to create a capital letter (using the SHIFT key), how to put spaces between the words with the SPACE bar, and how to delete any mistakes (with the BACKSPACE key). When they have completed their sentence, save the work to their individual folders to be printed at a more convenient time.

For reinforcement, ask the children to work on copies of the speech bubbles activities (**Bubbles 1.doc** to **Bubbles 2.doc**). Pairs should choose one of the four pictures and discuss what they think the characters are saying to each another. They can then type a sentence inside each speech bubble, save and print their work out.

At their desks

The children can practise their handwriting and letter formation by writing another sentence underneath those they have typed once they have been printed. Why not let them draw a picture to go with their sentences as well?

Give children printed copies of the speech bubbles activities for them to practise their handwriting skills on before they work at the computer.

Conclusion

Remind the children of the importance of using the SHIFT key to create a capital letter. Check that all the children are using this method rather than using CAPS LOCK. It is also important at this stage to check that the children are pressing the SPACE bar only once between words – you might find that children press it 3 or 4 times so it looks like a finger space! Encourage the children to describe any differences that they have found between written and typed text. Reinforce the idea that text can easily be entered and corrected on the computer using the keyboard.

Adapting the idea

❑ Why not type out messages to stick inside celebration cards, for birthdays, Easter, Christmas or Diwali?
❑ In other subjects, encourage children to type their work straight onto the computer rather than writing it. They can practise using the SPACE bar, SHIFT and BACKSPACE keys – remind them to use the full stop!

Try giving out copies of a keyboard (photocopy a real keyboard for quick and simple worksheets!) and asking children to find and colour the SPACE bar, SHIFT, BACKSPACE and full stop keys. They could also colour the keys needed to type their name or the name of the school.

Enter here

Introduction

Gather the whole class together and compare a piece of prose with a poem. Look at the differences in the layout and rhythm, but guide the children towards looking at the sentence structure. Talk about how sentences in a poem often start on a new line. Look at a selection of poems to see if this rule is true to all poems. The children will discover that all poems are different: some have rhyming words at the end of every line and some don't, some are funny and others describe things,but most poems start a new line with every sentence.

ICT objective

❑ To learn that the RETURN key is used to insert a line break.

Resources

You will need: access to *Microsoft WordPad*; copies of **Seaside.doc** and **Shadow.doc** from the CD; printed copies of **Seaside.doc** and **Shadow.doc**; examples of prose and poetry, stickers, writing and drawing materials.

What to do

Show the children a copy of **Seaside.doc** on the computer screen. Read it just as you would a normal poem, but encourage the children to notice that it hasn't got a new line for every sentence – this is a poem with a problem! Perhaps the poet wasn't a very good typist and didn't know how to make a new line, so just left them out! Ask the children if they can find a key on the keyboard that could put new lines in for them. Encourage a few children to come up to the computer and choose a key that they think might be the right one. If nobody guesses correctly give them a clue, for example explain that it is the fattest key on the keyboard, and that it is called the RETURN key. You will be amazed how quickly they will remember where it is and what it is used for if you let the children discover the key for themselves!

When they have found the right key, explain that they need to press it once to move down one line. The more times they press it the more lines it moves down. Remind the children that they only need to use it to start a new line, **not** at the end of the line when typing normally because the computer will move to the next line on its own. Type a simple sentence to show this. Choose a coloured sticker to put on the RETURN key to help any children who have difficulty remembering where it is on the keyboard.

At the computer

Open a copy of **Seaside.doc** from the CD into *WordPad*. Individually or in pairs, ask the children to look at the poem and to use the RETURN key to add new lines where they think they are necessary in the poem. Recap how to use the mouse to position the pointer between the words that need to be separated with a new line, then to click once with the left mouse button to put the cursor in the correct position before pressing the RETURN key to start a new line. When they have finished, the work can be saved to their individual folders and printed at a more convenient time. Copies of **Shadow.doc** can be used as a reinforcement or alternative piece of work.

At their desks

Print out copies of the poem once the children have edited it, and ask them to draw a picture to accompany the poem. These could form part of a display, or a class poetry book.

Conclusion

Can the children think of any other times when the ENTER/RETURN key could be used? (To start a new line, a new paragraph, to create a list or to write the address on a letter). Ask a child to find and describe the position and shape of the key.

Adapting the idea

❏ Lots of different activities can be quickly created so children can practise using the RETURN key. Type a shopping list on a single line rather than as a list so the children can press RETURN after every word to create the list (this also works with numbers, days of the week or months of the year).
❏ Try asking the children to write their own poems, or to write another verse for 'The Seaside' or 'My Shadow' (**Shadow.doc**) from the CD.
❏ Creating a set of instructions is a good way for the children to use the RETURN key – encourage the children to write a simple set of instructions in *WordPad* for looking after a pet, or write the instructions out ready for the children to divide up with the ENTER key.

And, and, and!

Introduction

Read the story of 'The Emperor's New Clothes' (**Emperor.doc** on the CD that accompanies this book) to the class. Read with all the 'and's and no full stops – see if the children notice that anything is wrong!

Encourage them to realise that the story was very difficult to read because you couldn't take a breath, and that it was very boring and repetitive. Show the children an enlarged printout of the story, and ask them if they can see what is missing. Highlight that a story doesn't sound very interesting if it says and, and, and, and, and! Explain that instead of 'and', we can use a full stop and a capital letter. This will make the story easier to read and more exciting!

ICT objectives

❏ To know that text can be entered and corrected.
❏ To be able to insert and delete text to improve work.

Resources

You will need: access to *Microsoft WordPad*; copies of **Emperor.doc** from the CD; printed copies of **Emperor.doc**; writing and drawing materials.

What to do

Explain to the children what you want them to do: edit the story, removing the 'and's, replacing them with full stops and new sentences starting with a capital letter.

Show the children the BACKSPACE key (usually found in the top right-hand corner of the keyboard marked with an arrow: ← and explain that this deletes things to the left of the cursor. Next show them the DELETE key (usually has 'Del' or 'Delete' written on it): this deletes letters to the right of the cursor.

Make sure they know that a full stop is always followed by a capital letter. Recap how to create capital letters, and remind the children where the keys are on the keyboard if they have forgotten.

At the computer

Individually or in pairs, ask children to open a copy of **Emperor.doc** into *WordPad* and let them work through the story, changing the words and adding punctuation.

When they have completed the task, save the work to their individual folders and print it out at a more convenient time.

At their desks

Once the work has been printed out, children can draw the Emperor wearing what they think his new clothes would have looked like at the bottom of the page. Would they be brightly coloured?

Conclusion

Read the original version of 'The Emperor's New Clothes' from the CD to the class (or ask a more confident child to read) and discuss what is wrong with it. Then ask a child to read their altered version; how does it differ from the original? Has anyone added new words to the text? Discuss and revise any difficulties that were encountered.

Adapting the idea

❑ If the story is too difficult for some of the children to read, concentrate on just a few sentences, asking them to read and alter these rather than struggling through the whole story.

❑ More confident children could think of words which replace 'and' to connect two sentences, such as 'therefore' or 'because'.

❑ The children could revise all the skills they have learned in this chapter by creating a class book. There are lots of different types of books that the children could create: fiction or non-fiction, science fiction, adventure stories, or books about animals or plants. They could type the story into the computer, and when it has been printed they could draw a picture to go with it. Once every child or group has completed a page, arrange them into a class book with a contents page and an index.

Workshops

How to create your own speech bubbles activities

The speech bubbles activities can be great fun for children, and it is easy to create scenes using Clip Art images that will fit with any topic work you may be doing.

Resources

You will need: access to *Microsoft Word*; suitable Clip Art images (those used in the speech bubbles activities can be found in the 'Workshop components' folder on the CD).

What to do

Open up *Microsoft Word* and create a new document. Make sure you can see the whole page on the screen (click *View > Page Layout*, then set 'Zoom' to 'Whole page') to give you a blank page to work on.

Adding the picture of the scene is easy: just insert your choice of Clip Art or another picture to the page by clicking *Insert > Picture >*

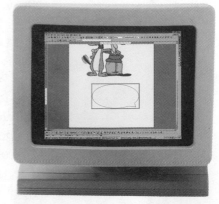

From File and choosing the picture you want to use (to use an image from a Clip Art gallery, choose *Insert > Picture > Clip Art*). Once the image is on the page, you can resize it and position it as you wish by pointing to the image and clicking with the left mouse button, then adjusting the size with the handles that appear around the edge of the image.

If you have trouble moving the image once it has been added to the page, right-click on the image, and select 'Format picture' from the menu that appears. In the 'Format picture' dialogue box, click the 'Position' tab and make sure that there is a tick next to 'Float over text'. Click 'OK' and you should be able to move the image freely about the page.

The speech bubbles are created using the 'AutoShapes' tool on the 'Drawing' toolbar. Click *Draw > AutoShapes > Callouts*, then select the 'Speech Bubble' tool and draw two speech bubbles by 'clicking and dragging' with the mouse. Move them into position above the characters, adjusting if you wish the direction of the pointer by clicking on the small yellow diamond that appears by the point and dragging it to a new position. Draw as many speech bubbles as are necessary for the scene.

To make sure that when the children type into the speech bubbles the text appears at the right size, click inside a speech bubble so that the flashing cursor appears. You can now alter the font, style, size and colour of any text that will be typed into the speech bubble.

Save the file to your folder ready for the children to use in the lesson.

Select 'Float over text' to make sure that the picture can be resized and moved independently.

8 : Picture this

Vocabulary and definitions

Brush tool: similar to the pencil tool; draws lines and shapes of different thickness, styles and colours.

Flood fill: to fill enclosed areas of the screen with a selected colour.

Graphics: different images displayed on the computer. These can be drawings, photos, lines, charts, animations or video.

Icon: small pictures or symbols displayed on the screen to represent a file, folder or application.

Line tool: used to draw straight and diagonal lines of different thickness and colours.

Pencil tool: draws freehand lines and shapes of different colours, much the same as a real pencil.

Save As: saving a file with a different name or format, so the original is preserved and a copy is made.

Spray tool: creates an effect similar to spray paint on the screen.

Texture: creating a paint effect using different combinations of the program's tools.

Project overview
Creating pictures

Project	Subject link	ICT objective
Woodcuts	Art	To practise mark-making
Yellow islands	Art	To create and explore colour
Make your own Mondrian	Art	To make geometric images

CD resources

These activities are located in the 'Picture this' folder on the CD that accompanies this book. All the files will open in *Microsoft Paint,* which comes as standard with all versions of *Windows,* and can usually be found by clicking *Start > Programs > Accessories > Paint.*

The files you will need are called **Flood fill.bmp**, **Mondrian.bmp**, **Replace.bmp**, **Woodcut.bmp** and **Yellow islands.bmp**.

Creating pictures

Using the computer to generate graphics, images and pictures is one of the most exciting aspects of using ICT in the classroom – with only a few mouse clicks children are able to create works of art and striking effects quickly and effectively.

There are many computer applications that allow the user to paint and draw, ranging from simple paint programs such as *Microsoft Paint*, to those that allow sophisticated effects and the creation of 3-D pictures (such as *Adobe PhotoShop* or *3-D Studio*). More complicated 'grown-up' applications allow images to be manipulated and completely transformed, but almost all paint applications have a basic set of tools and functions: Brush, Pen, Fill, Line, Shape, Eraser and Marquee, for example, are common to most programs, but will have various options to create different effects. At this level, children need only to become familiar with these basic tools and what they can do with them, so advanced features are not really necessary. In the infant classroom, a copy of *Paint* will be more than adequate for most needs.

Another thing to remember when working with graphics on a computer is that images can exist in many different formats: JPEG, Bitmap, Tiff, GIF, and many more. To us, whatever the format, the picture will look the same, but not to the computer. The format of the image indicates the way the image information is stored on the computer, and as a result the way it is read by the program. Think of different file formats as different languages – some programs will read many different file formats, some won't. Some will save images in one format, while others save in another. Most, though, will allow you to choose the format of the final image. This issue of format is important when obtaining images from other sources, such as the Internet, a scanner or digital camera, as they will all save images in a different way. You need to make sure that the file format they use is compatible with the software you will be using, otherwise the two will be incompatible.

Finally, the size of an image is important, both in terms of its dimensions (in centimetres) and the amount of disk space taken up by the file (in kilobytes). An image may only be 10cm by 10cm on your computer display, but the computer may still be thinking of it as a scanned A4 photo, so there will be a lot of wasted information that isn't displayed. Reducing the physical dimensions of the image will reduce how much disk space the image will consume without altering the way it looks on the screen. Considering this when dealing with images will save a lot of headaches when trying to save images to disk, import them into documents or upload them to a web page.

Windows has a very simple, yet versatile graphics program called *Paint* that is supplied as standard. It can be found by clicking *Start > Programs > Accessories > Paint*. Using *Paint* in the classroom has two main advantages: if you have *Windows* you have already got it, and the chances are the children will also have it at home, making their skills transferable and allowing them to practise at home. The activities in this chapter will be based around *Paint*, but they can easily be modified for any graphics package that you might be using.

A note about copyright

Be warned that simply copying images from a website or CD-ROM, even if only for use in the primary classroom, may constitute a breach of copyright along the same lines as photocopying extracts from books. It would be a good idea to check your school's policy and position with regard to images and copyright before setting research tasks for the children.

Before you start

Before allowing the children to use *Paint*, it may be useful to do a bit of preparation to make sure that when children start *Paint*, it starts in a way that they can use straight away. Here's a checklist:

Make sure *Paint* opens in a full window. Click on the 'Maximise' button: 🔲 to expand the window as large as it will go, then click the 'Close' button: ☒. When *Paint* is reopened, it will open in a full window.

The 'paper' area (the white space in which you can draw) may not fit the window and may look something like the screen in the

Maximise the space in which the children can draw by resizing the canvas.

diagram.This can easily be changed. Around the white area there will be small black squares. Point at the square in the bottom-right corner with the mouse until the pointer changes to a double-headed arrow: ⬉. Click the left mouse button and drag the area until it fills the screen; when you release the mouse button, the paper area should have increased in size.

Make sure that the toolbar and colour palette are visible. If they are not, click *View*, and make sure there are ticks by 'Tool box' and 'Color box'; the palettes should appear on the screen. Having made any changes, close *Paint*, then re-open it to see if the changes have taken effect.

These simple checks before a lesson can save a lot of time and frustration!

Skills practice

Opening *Paint*

Before tackling the projects in this chapter, children should be familiar with accessing *Paint*. If they have covered the activities in Chapter 1, 'Introducing mouse control', they may already be familiar with this.

Ask children to open and close *Paint* by accessing it through the *Start* menu. Extend this by asking children to access particular print files directly from their own folder, as shown in the 'File handling and desktop management' chapter.

The toolbar

Before working on any projects, the children need time to get used to the features of the tools on the toolbar. The following practice activities will introduce children to each tool individually. Carry these activities out over a number of sessions to allow children time to practise with the tools individually. It may be useful to make a large display of the *Paint* toolbar that can be used by the class as a reference point for their work.

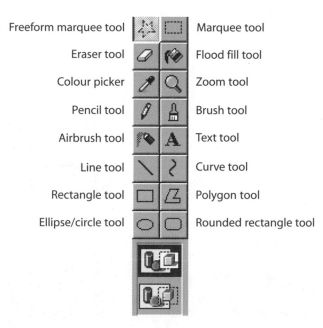

Freeform marquee tool			Marquee tool
Eraser tool			Flood fill tool
Colour picker			Zoom tool
Pencil tool			Brush tool
Airbrush tool			Text tool
Line tool			Curve tool
Rectangle tool			Polygon tool
Ellipse/circle tool			Rounded rectangle tool

Remind the children to click on the screen with the left mouse button to make a mark, and to 'click and drag' with the left mouse button pressed down to draw a shape using these tools. Moving the pointer without the mouse button pressed allows them to move the tool to where they want without making a mark.

All these activities are broadly similar, and can easily be adapted to fit within a topic by varying the theme of what they are asked to do. In these examples, children are simply asked to scribble patterns, but specific objectives or tasks could be set.

Pencil tool

Identify the Pencil tool on the toolbar (see diagram above), and demonstrate how to use it by selecting the tool, then choosing a colour from the palette at the bottom of the screen before pointing to the blank canvas, clicking with the left mouse button and drawing

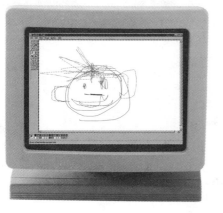

with the mouse as if it were a pencil. While the left mouse button is pressed, the pencil on the screen will leave a trail following the movements of the mouse.

Children could just freely explore using this tool if you wish, but it is more effective if they have a focused task. For example, ask them to select the pencil tool and make scribble patterns. They have to make five scribble patterns in five different colours in five minutes.

Scribble pictures like that on the left will be produced. Once children have created their image they can print it out or save it to their folder.

Brush tool

The technique for using the brush tool is similar to that described above for the pencil tool. With the brush, though, there are extra options that allow you to change the size of line that you draw. When selecting the brush tool, another palette of brush styles will appear underneath the toolbox (see left), which allows you to change the size and shape of the paintbrush. Repeat the above activity, this time using

the brush tool to create similar scribble patterns (see below right), and encouraging the children to choose different brush styles as well as colours.

Try also drawing lines with the different brushes, so that each brush mark can be compared.

Airbrush tool

Choosing this tool also brings up a set of options providing a choice of brush sizes. Ask children to create their scribble patterns again, but this time ask them to observe the difference between holding the airbrush in one place and moving it about the screen. Holding it in one place allows colour to be concentrated, while moving the pointer around the screen at various speeds while holding the left mouse button

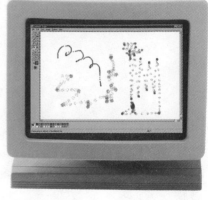

down creates a more textured effect (see right). Ask the children to create scribble pictures using three sizes and three different colours, showing fast and slow movements with the mouse.

Different drawing tools

When the children have all had a chance to carry out these three activities, ask them if they can think of any differences or similarities between the patterns they made with each of the three tools. Did their scribble patterns look different? How were they different? Are these differences the same as if they were using a real paintbrush or pencil?

Flood fill tool

This tool will 'flood' an area with the colour chosen from the palette at the bottom of the screen. The file **Flood fill.bmp** on the CD will be useful to help children practise this. Ask children to take a copy of this file, then select the flood fill tool and a colour. By placing the pointer in an area of the image and clicking once with the left mouse button, that area will then be filled with the selected colour. Bear in mind that the area has to be enclosed by a coloured line, otherwise the whole area will be flooded – this can be demonstrated if children try to fill one of the segments in the top-left corner: the whole of the surrounding area will be flooded because there are gaps in the lines. Children can undo any mistakes by clicking *Edit > Undo*.

Ask children to practise filling the spaces in **Flood fill.bmp**, and set them a challenge: see if they can fill all the segments of the image, with no two segments next to one another filled with the same colour.

The flood fill tool is quite powerful, as whole areas can be flooded with colour at a stroke. Try and encourage the children not to have heavily coloured backgrounds in their artwork, as this will use up a lot of your printer ink. This happens especially when children are asked to make Christmas cards: the first thing they do is fill the page in black so that they can illustrate snow! It is worthwhile exploring alternative ways of doing this with children, using the tools available to create the necessary effects. Managing computer paint activities like this will save you a lot of printer ink.

Shape tools

The rectangle, rounded rectangle and circle tools each work in a similar way. To draw a shape, click the appropriate button on the toolbar. When a shape tool is selected the following options are available:

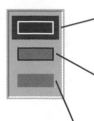

This option allows children to draw an outlined shape with the outline colour selected from the palette at the bottom of the screen. To draw the shape, position the pointer at one corner of the shape, click the left mouse button and drag the mouse to the opposite corner of the shape. Release the mouse button to finish drawing the shape.

The second option allows children to draw two-colour shapes. The first colour is chosen with the left mouse button (this will be the line colour); the second colour will be the fill colour, and is chosen by clicking with the right mouse button on another colour in the palette. The colour indicator will show both colours, and by 'clicking and dragging' with the mouse as before, they can create the shape. Remind children to return the background to white by right-clicking on white in the palette at the bottom of the screen, otherwise when they use the eraser tool, the wrong colour may be erased.

The third option allows children to create solid shapes. The colour of the shape will be the one chosen with the right mouse button, as it was with the previous tool.

If you want to draw perfect circles or squares with these tools, hold down the SHIFT key while drawing the shape.

Ask the children to use the tools to create a picture using all three types of shape, and different colours for each shape they draw.

Polygon tool

The polygon tool allows you to draw a multi-sided shape (although not regular polygons). It works slightly differently to the other shape tools: click, hold and drag the mouse to draw the first side of the shape, then release the mouse button and repeat to draw the next side, continuing until the shape is completed. Double-click the left mouse button when all the sides are complete, and the shape will be filled with colour (if you have chosen either of the solid shape options). To restrict the sides to only 45- and 90-degree angles, hold down SHIFT while dragging the mouse to draw the side. The options for drawing solid, two-colour and outline shapes are the same as for the regular shapes. Ask the children to practise creating a star shape using this tool, using different colours to create solid and hollow stars.

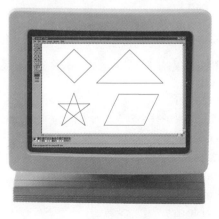

Line tool

This tool draws simple straight lines of various colours and sizes on the screen by pointing with the mouse. To create a line children need to choose a colour and line thickness from the toolbars, then 'click and drag' with the mouse from the start to the

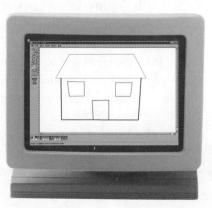

finish of the line. Ask the children to create an image using just lines (see previous page). Encourage them to use as many different colours, styles and angles of line as they can.

Curve tool

This tool is similar to the line tool, but slightly more complicated to use. With a little practice, though, it is easily mastered. Select the curve tool, then line thickness and colour as for a normal line. 'Click and drag' with the mouse to draw the start and end points of the curve, then use the pointer to 'pull' the line into a curve by 'clicking and dragging'; the line should bend and follow the movement of the pointer. Release the mouse button when you are happy with the curve. If you want to add another bend to the line, 'click and drag' again to produce an 'S' shaped curve, or double-click with the mouse to finish drawing the curve. This is not an easy skill to teach, and practice is the best way to work out how to achieve the best results – remember if a line goes wrong, you can click *Edit > Undo* to remove the line and start again.

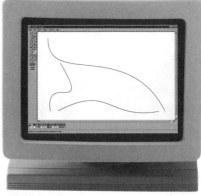

Eraser tool

Children find this tool quite self-explanatory, given that it is the one they can most easily relate to a 'real' context. To 'rub out' anything on the screen select the eraser tool, choose an eraser size from the toolbar that appears, then use the mouse as you would the paintbrush to move the cursor over the area to be erased.

This tool has more advanced features than a simple eraser: it can be used to replace selected colours on an image. To illustrate this useful feature, use a copy of the file **Replace.bmp**.

Show the children the image on the screen, and ask them how they could get rid of all the red from the image, replacing it with yellow. Do they think this is possible? Choose the eraser tool, then use the left mouse button to select the colour you want to replace (in this case red) and the right mouse button to select the colour you want to replace it with (yellow). Now select the largest eraser size. To replace all the red in the picture with yellow, click and hold the right mouse button as you move the pointer over the image: you will see any red the mouse passes over turn to yellow rather than being erased – the other colours will remain untouched. You have made an 'intelligent' eraser.

Ask the children to work to replace all the green on the image with a colour of their choice. Remind them to use the right mouse button, otherwise they will replace everything with the colour they have selected. Also remind them to right-click on white to return the eraser to its original state when they have finished.

Once children have completed any or all of the above practice activities they can be printed out so they can record what they have done and their observations. These can then be used as the children's own individual reference manuals when they use *Paint* to create images.

After introducing these skills, make sure you allow children opportunities to practise what they have learned. Every time you ask the class to create a picture or diagram, make the computer available as an option. Using a filing system like that described in the 'File handling and desktop management' chapter will allow children the opportunity to save their work and gradually build up their images. This reduces the amount of time children need to spend on the computer in any one session, and can allow you to set time limits in which they can work.

Projects

Woodcuts

Introduction

Before working at the computer, the children will need to have had experience of various examples of woodcuts and other works of art. The work of MC Escher or Jackson Pollock would be a good starting point for children to look at how mark-making can create patterns, and for them to think about how these could be recreated using the computer.

ICT objective

❏ To be able to select and use simple mark-making tools in a paint package.

Resources

You will need: access to *Microsoft Paint*; copies of **Woodcut.bmp** from the CD; a selection of pictures illustrating woodcuts (some good examples can be found at www.godecookery.com/clipart/clart.htm); black and white paper, black and white paints and crayons.

What to do

Show the children some examples of woodcut images, either from books or from an online source (see Resources). Discuss the woodcuts with the children, and ask them whether they think they were drawn as white on black, or black on white. Which would be easier to draw? What differences are there between the two methods?

Tell the children that they are going to use the computer to make their own woodcuts. Show them a copy of **Woodcut.bmp**, and briefly recap how to use the paintbrush tool to make marks on the screen in either black or white, as if they were making a woodcut themselves. What are the differences in drawing on the two different backgrounds? Try to show that to achieve the same result on both backgrounds, you need to add to one and take away from the other.

At the computer

Ask the children to create their own woodcuts using the computer and a blank copy of **Woodcut.bmp**. In the left-hand square, they should use a white paintbrush to draw a simple object such as a flower. In the right-hand square, encourage them to do the reverse, selecting the Brush tool and black to use on the white background.

Once children have completed their woodcuts, save the files to the children's individual folders. They can be printed out for display, or can be used as a desktop background image (see the 'File handling and desktop management' chapter for details on how to do this).

At their desks

Ask the children to use the painting and drawing materials to try making black and white 'woodcut' images like they will do on the screen using paper and paints or crayons. Can they create images similar to those that they created using the computer?

Conclusion

Ask the children to compare their work with woodcuts created using traditional methods, and to discuss the effectiveness of their work – was it easier or harder than they thought it would be using the computer? How do they think they would make a woodcut in real life? What did they like or dislike about the various methods they used at the computer?

Adapting the idea

❑ Encourage children to create a woodcut image from scratch. Ask them to open *Paint* and to use the flood fill tool to fill the background with a colour of their choice, then to use the paintbrush, Pencil and airbrush tools in a contrasting colour to create their image.
❑ Try asking children to use the Eraser tool to create their image, so they are 'rubbing out' the background rather than painting on top of it. Does this create a different kind of effect, or is it just a different way to create the same kind of image?

Yellow islands

Introduction

Show the class a copy of Jackson Pollock's *Yellow Islands* (you can find copies of this picture in reference books or from the Tate Gallery). How do the children think the painting was created? Was it created using a computer? Do they think the rhythmic pattern of flowing black lines could be recreated using the mouse and computer? Ask the children what other colours they can see and why they think the painting is called *Yellow Islands*.

ICT objectives

❏ To allow children to use the Fill tool to create highlights of colour.
❏ To use 'Save As' to save work, allowing children to save different versions of their work.

Resources

You will need: access to *Microsoft Paint*; copies of **Yellow islands.bmp** from the CD; a copy of Jackson Pollock's *Yellow Islands* (this can be found in textbooks, or from the Tate Gallery); writing and drawing materials.

What to do

Open a copy of **Yellow islands.bmp** using *Paint*, and show the file to the children as a class. This is an image in the style of Jackson Pollock's 'Yellow Islands', but is missing any additional colours – this is what the children are going to add to the image to create their own version of Pollock's original.

Tell the children that they are going to modify their own copy of the image using *Paint* to add colour to try and recreate the feel of Jackson Pollock's original. They can do this by filling areas of the image with another colour using the flood fill tool, or by drawing other islands on the picture with the paintbrush tool.

Ask the children, using a copy of the original image as a reference, what they think they would need to add to the picture to recreate the feel of the original *Yellow Islands* painting. Ask them to think how they could do this using a computer and the drawing tools that they have been learning to use. Encourage them to think about the effects they could use to alter the image they can see on the screen.

Recap the different tools that are available in *Paint* and how to use them to make marks and shapes on the screen. Demonstrate a few of their suggested changes using the copy of **Yellow islands.bmp** on the screen.

At the computer

Children can now work individually on their own copy of **Yellow islands.bmp** to modify the file using the basic tools in *Paint*. Remind them of the ideas and techniques they discussed earlier, and if necessary how to use the tools in *Paint*. They may wish to create more than one version of the file to try different ideas out, so allow them to use the 'Save As' function to create multiple copies of the file with a different file name. Remind them that if they had called this new file by the same name, or had just used 'Save' then they would have lost their original image and they wouldn't be able to compare the two.

If necessary, show the children how to save work using 'Save As': click *File > Save As*, then choose a folder to save the image in to, and choose a new file name for the image. (This is covered in more detail in the 'File handling and desktop management' chapter.)

At their desks

Ask the children, either individually or in groups, to try and use collage materials and paints to create an image in the style of Jackson Pollock, using the materials to make marks on paper.

Conclusion

Print off copies of the children's work when they have finished making their changes. Ask them to record details of what changes they made, how they made them, and to make comparisons with Pollock's original painting, detailing what they like about the images they have made and what they would change.

Adapting the idea

Use printouts of all the children's work to create a class gallery display of their work inspired by Jackson Pollock.

Ask the children to use *Paint's* tools to create images using lines and colours to express a variety of themes with contrast between colours, such as 'Fireworks' or 'The motorway at night'. The children could provide their own titles that show how they used lines and colours.

Make your own Mondrian

Introduction

Piet Mondrian (1872–1944), was a Dutch painter who created abstract images using simple lines and colours. His bold geometric designs are striking, and children can easily recreate them using the computer.

There are many websites that show pictures of Mondrian's work. A great many examples can be found at www.artchive.com. This activity allows children to add the their own colours to a Mondrian 'original', which has been created using *Paint* to look like part of Mondrian's *Composition with Large Blue Plane, Red, Black, Yellow, and Gray*.

ICT objectives

❏ To allow children to use the Fill tool and shape tools to create areas of colour and to create images with a geometric theme.
❏ To use the 'Save As ' function to save work, allowing children to save different versions of their work.

Resources

You will need: access to *Microsoft Paint*; copies of **Mondrian.bmp** from the CD; examples of art work by Mondrian (these are available in textbooks, or from www.artchive.com).

What to do

Look together at some examples of Mondrian's work, and ask the children what they like about the pictures they are looking at – do they like the colours? The shapes? Do they think they could recreate Mondrian's work using a computer, based on what skills they have been learning so far in this chapter?

Once children have looked at and discussed the elements of Mondrian's work, tell them that they are going to use the computer to make their own Mondrian image.

There are two simple ways for children to create their own Mondrian images using *Paint*; each uses a different technique, but produces a similar effect. The children can use the one that they are most comfortable with, comparing the two methods at the end of the activity to see which is their favourite. Demonstrate the methods to the children using a copy of *Paint*.

Method 1

Open a copy of **Mondrian.bmp** in *Paint*, and show the children the grid of lines. Can they see any similarities between this and Mondrian's work? What's missing? Do the children know of any way that they could use *Paint* to add colour to the file?

Demonstrate how to use the flood fill tool to add colour to areas of **Mondrian.bmp**, to make a picture in the style of Mondrian. Remember to vary the choice of colours, and to leave some sections white in order to maintain a contrast.

Method 2

This method uses the filled rectangle option on a blank page in *Paint*. Show children how to use the filled rectangle tool to create solid shapes of different colours. Remember to use the right mouse button to select the colour of the solid shape, and to set the outline of the shape to black by selecting from the palette with the left mouse button. 'Click and drag' on the blank page to create solid shapes in a variety of colours, trying to overlap the shapes in the style of Mondrian.

Once you have demonstrated both methods, tell the children that they will now have the opportunity to use either of these methods to create their own image in the style of Mondrian.

At the computer

Individually or in pairs, set the children to work on creating a Mondrian image using either of the methods described above. If they choose to use method 1, they will need their own blank copy of Mondrian.bmp, otherwise a blank canvas will do.

If they want to create different images, or to try out different methods of working, tell them to use the 'Save As' function to save different copies of their work to their folder so that they can return to them at a later date, and see their favourite ideas again.

Conclusion

When children have finished working at the computer, print their work out and encourage them to compare it with pictures of Mondrian's work. What is similar? What is different? Which image do they prefer, and which method of creating an image did they find easiest? Ask children to look at their designs and give them titles in the style Mondrian style, such as *A big blue square with red and yellow bits*, and to explain how they created the picture using the computer.

Adapting the idea

❏ Try creating similar images using different shapes – circles can create some striking designs, and are easy to draw in *Paint*.
❏ When children have printed their images, they can be cut out and used on cards or to decorate things they have made. This can be further extended by using the special papers available for printers, including T-shirt paper that allows children to iron their images onto clothing or stickers, and even magnetic paper to make fridge magnets!

9 : Animated books

Vocabulary and definitions

Animation: a movement of an individual piece of text or a picture on the computer screen.

Presentation: a collection of animated 'pages' combining text, images and sound together on the computer screen that the user can work through.

Slides: a single 'page' of a presentation.

Stories that move

This chapter has been created just for teachers. It provides a step-by-step guide through the simple process of creating an animated book. Animated stories can be any popular book or poem created using the computer, using moving text, pictures and sounds to create an exciting visual display. There are two examples of animated stories on the CD that accompanies this book to demonstrate the kind of things that are possible – both have been created using *Microsoft PowerPoint* and Clip Art that is freely available from many sources. Any story you like can be created by manipulating text, Clip Art and sound files with a little know-how: simple repeated animation settings and sounds can be added to each picture or piece of text to build up a rhythmic structure to a story.

These animated books make a good alternative to Big Books and, when used in conjunction with a data projector, can be used in front of the whole class for shared reading.

The following workshop will give stage-by-stage instructions showing how to create an animated story entitled 'The old house'. A copy of the finished presentation is on the CD in the 'Animated books' folder so you can see what the workshop will produce, and all the components that have been used in the workshop are in the 'Workshop components' folder to allow you to follow the instructions step by step.

Also on the CD is another animated book entitled 'Hickory dickory dock', which provides another example of what can be created using *PowerPoint*; feel free to use this file in lessons, and to open it in *PowerPoint* to see how all the different effects have been created.

Both the *PowerPoint* presentations will open in any edition of *PowerPoint* from *PowerPoint 97* onwards. To get the most from these stories, you will need a computer that is capable of playing sound, and some means of presenting the story to the whole class at once – either on a large monitor, or through a projector that will put your presentation on a large blank area of wall for the class to see.

Project

The old house

Introduction

The best way to see how this file has been created is to look at the copy of **The old house.ppt** that is on the CD, and to see what settings have been used in order to create these finished effects. The instructions that follow will explain how these have been created. Please note that these instructions have been written using *Microsoft PowerPoint 97* and although other versions of the software are similar, there may be slight differences between the options and screenshots shown here and your particular version of *PowerPoint*.

The Clip Art files on the CD will need copying to a folder on your hard disk before you insert them into the presentation. This can be done using the menu program on the CD; make sure you know where to find the Clip Art images once you've copied them to the hard disk!

Resources

You will need: access to *Microsoft PowerPoint*; a copy of **The old house.ppt** from the CD as an example to follow; the Clip Art and sounds from the 'Workshop components' folder on the CD; a multimedia computer.

What to do

Setting the background

Open *Microsoft PowerPoint* and, from the first list of options, choose to start a 'Blank presentation', then click 'OK'. From the second list of options choose 'Blank' (the bottom right-hand option) and click 'OK'. This will present you with a blank screen, or 'slide', on which to work (see above).

To set the background of the slide to something other than plain white, click with the right mouse button anywhere on the blank slide, and select 'Background' from the menu that appears.

Click on the down arrow at the bottom of the screen to bring up a palette of colour choices for the background. From this, choose the colour you want to use as the backdrop for the story, or click 'More colours' or 'Fill effects' to choose from a more comprehensive set of

Click on the down arrow to choose a colour from the palette.

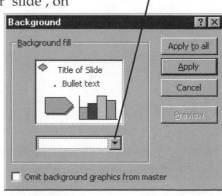

colours. 'Fill effects' allows you to add textures, patterns and fades to your background – experiment with these to see what effects they can produce, or simply pick a solid colour. For a scary story about a spooky house, choose a dark colour. When you are happy with your choice of colour (you can see a preview of what it will look like in the dialogue box), click 'Apply to all' so that all new slides will have the same background. If you click 'Apply', only the slide you are currently working on will have this background, and you'll have to repeat this process for all new slides.

Before you move on, it is a good idea to save your work so you can go back to it should anything go wrong, or you make a mistake. Select *File > Save,* select a folder to save the work in to and type in the name of your presentation. (See the 'File handling and desktop management' chapter for more information on saving files to specific folders.) Keep saving the presentation after each step by clicking on the disk icon on the top toolbar, ▪.

Adding a picture

To add the spooky house picture to the first slide of the presentation, click *Insert > Picture > From file* on the toolbar at the top of the screen. In the dialogue box that appears, use the 'Look in' drop-down menu to select the folder your Clip Art images are kept in, then choose the image **Haunted house.gif**. Click 'OK' to add the image to the slide.

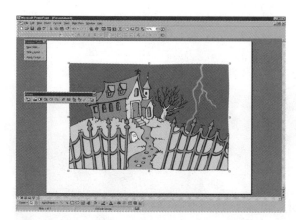

Once the picture is on the slide, it may not be the right size, or in the right place. Use the mouse and click once with the left button on the image to select it: eight boxes should appear around the edge of the image. Point to any of the four corners and the cursor should change to a 'resize' arrow: ↘. Click with the left mouse button, hold and drag the corner of the picture until it is the right size, filling the screen.

When a picture has been inserted, 'click and drag' the boxes that appear around the image to move it in to the correct position.

Adding text

Once the picture is in place the story's title can be placed on top of the image. Select the text box tool: ▣ from the 'Drawing' toolbar at the bottom of the page (if you can't see the 'Drawing' toolbar, click *View > Toolbars* and select 'Drawing'). Using the mouse, point to where you want the text box to go, then hold down the left mouse button and drag the pointer to create a text box. Make sure the box is wide enough to hold your text (although you can change this later), but don't worry about the depth of the box, as *PowerPoint* will adjust this automatically.

9: Animated books

When the box has been created, a flashing cursor will appear in it. Select the text type you require. Before you add text to the box, it is a good idea to set the font, size, style and colour of the text as you want it to appear on the screen. Use the drop-down menus and style buttons on the 'Formatting' toolbar to change these: pick the font of your choice (the more scary the better!), then alter the size (80pt is good for the title page, but 48pt is better for normal text).

Type in the book title 'The old house'. The text should appear as you styled it, and the size of the text box should change automatically. You may need to move the text box if it has appeared in the wrong place. To do this, click once on the text with the left mouse button, then point to the shaded border around the text. The cursor should change to a cross: ⁺. Click the left mouse button, hold it down, and drag with the mouse to move the text box to where you want it to be, then release the left mouse button.

Animating the slide

The layout of the front page is complete, but before it will animate you need to tell the slide what to do by adding the animation settings.

This small thumbnail image of the slide will show you which element of the slide you are changing the animation settings for, and will allow you to preview any animation settings you change.

This box shows whether an object will be animatated or not, and the order in which this will happen. Objects on the slide that are not animated can be seen in the 'Timing' section below.

This box shows how the item will animate. The window to the right of this allows you to set whether animated text appears word by word, letter by letter or all at once.

This box allows you to add a sound effect to accompany the animation, choosing either the sound effects included with *PowerPoint*, or by adding your own files.

This section allows you to remove objects after animation, but is not used in this workshop.

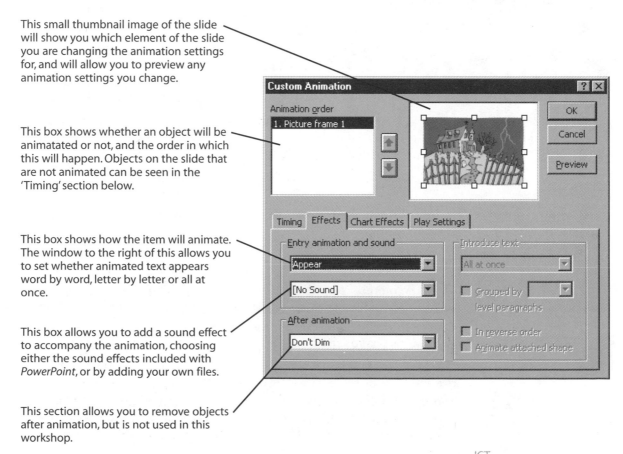

Using the right mouse button, click anywhere on the haunted house picture. Select 'Custom Animation' from the menu that pops up. The 'Custom Animation' dialogue box will appear, which will look something like the screenshot below.

The 'Effects' section at the bottom of the box dictates how the object will come onto the screen – for example whether it zooms in, flies from the top or crawls from either side of the screen. It also allows you to control whether there are any sounds that accompany the animation, and whether text appears word by word, letter by letter, or all at once.

In the top-left box, 'Picture frame 1' (which is the picture) will already be listed. This shows that the object will be animated, and when highlighted shows that the settings in the 'Effects' box relate to that object.

To make the haunted house picture (Picture frame 1) appear like a pair of blinds, select 'Blinds' in the left-hand box; to decide which way to make the blinds open, select 'Horizontal' in the box next to it. Click the 'Preview' button to see a sample of what this will look like.

Animating the text is a similar process. In the 'Timing' section, click on 'Text 2' and select 'Animate' to signify that the object should be animated – it will appear in the top left-hand box. Now highlight 'Text 2'

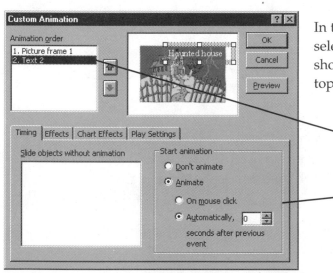

This box shows which objects will be animated, and the order in which this will happen.

These options control when the animation will happen – whether you have to click with the mouse in order to make it happen. Any objects that are not animated are listed on the left.

and choose 'Fly From Left' in the 'Effects' section. Click 'Preview' and you should see the two stages of animation. Because you are animating text, it is also possible to choose how the text appears: all at once, by word, or letter by letter. The box on the right allows you to change this; in this case, choose 'All at once'.

Next you have to tell the computer when to animate each of the elements of the slide – whether it happens automatically, or whether you have to click the mouse in order to move on. The 'Timing' section allows you to change this. Click on the 'Timing' section. This allows you to change the order in which the slide objects are animated, based on the order in the window at the top of the dialogue box.

9: Animated books

Click on 'Picture frame 1' in the list at the top, and then select 'Automatically' from the options next to it. This tells the computer to animate the picture (as you defined earlier) as soon as you start the slide show. To animate the text, click on 'Text 2' in the list, and select 'Automatically' again so that the text follows the picture without you having to do anything.

The slide is now animated. Click 'Preview' to see how it will look.

Adding sound

To add sound to any of the objects as they animate, look under the 'Effects' section of the 'Custom Animation' dialogue box. Underneath the options that you set earlier telling the objects how to animate is another box which should say '[No Sound]' at the moment.

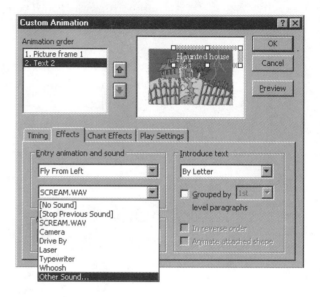

Select 'Picture frame 1' from the list at the top of the screen, then click the arrow next to '[No Sound]'. Scroll to the bottom of the list of pre-defined sound options and choose 'Other sound...', which will bring up a dialogue box where you can choose the sound effect to accompany the animation of the picture. Locate the folder in which you have put the Clip Art for this workshop, and choose **Swish.wav**. When you click 'OK', you will hear a preview of the sound.

This slide doesn't need any other sounds, and all the other animation settings have been fixed, so click 'OK' to return to the slide. Your first slide is now complete.

Checking the first slide

To see what the slide looks like, click the 'Slide Show' icon in the bottom-left of the screen and everything should happen automatically. When the animation has finished, click once with the left mouse button anywhere on the screen; it will go black with the instructions 'End of slide show, click to exit'. Click again with the left mouse button to return to the editing screen. Once you are happy that everything is working correctly, save your work before carrying on.

Click this button to run the slide show, or click *View > Slide Show*.

Creating the second slide

The steps that created the first slide are generally the same for all subsequent slides, but some minor details will be slightly different.

To add the second slide, click *Insert > New Slide* from the top toolbar. Select 'Blank' then click 'OK'; a new slide will appear, and it should already have a coloured background like the previous slide.

Add the picture of the door by clicking *Insert > Picture > From file*, then locating the Clip Art folder as before and choosing **Door.gif**. Position the image and resize it by 'clicking and dragging' with the mouse as you did for the image on the first slide.

Using the text box tool, add the text to the slide (see 'Adding text', above), styling the text as you wish (48pt is a good size for text on these slides). The text for the first slide is:

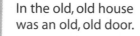

In the old, old house
was an old, old door.

To animate the objects on the slide, right-click on the text box and select 'Custom Animation' to bring up the 'Custom Animation' dialogue box. In the 'Timing' section, select 'Text 2' so that it appears in the list at the top, and set the animation settings to 'Fly From Top' in the 'Effects' section. No sound needs to accompany this animation, so leave the sound setting as '[No Sound]'. To make the text appear word by word, select 'By Word' in the 'Introduce text' section.

In the top-left box, put a tick next to 'Object 1' (which is the door picture) to animate this as well; the settings need to be 'Stretch' and 'From Right', and the sound needs to be added by selecting 'Other Sounds...' from the drop-down menu and choosing **Creak.wav** from the dialogue box that appears.

Now you need to tell the objects when to animate, so select the 'Timing' section. All the objects should be listed in the top left because you have already chosen to animate them; both should be set to animate automatically by clicking the 'Automatically' button on the right. However, they may be in the wrong order: the text should animate *before* the door, so the order may need to be changed.

The list in the box in the top left, when read from top to bottom, shows the order in which animated objects on a slide will appear. By clicking on an item in the list you can change this order with the 'Move up' and 'Move down' buttons next to the box. In this case, 'Text 2' wants to be above 'Picture frame 1' in the list, so click once with the left mouse button to highlight 'Text 2', then click with the left mouse button on the 'Move up' button to change the order of the list. You can click 'Preview' to see that the order is correct. When you are happy, click 'OK' to return to the main screen.

Select an object and use these buttons to move them up and down the list to change the order of the animation.

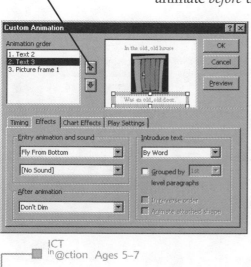

9: Animated books

To see the slide show so far, press PAGE UP to go to the first slide (PAGE UP and PAGE DOWN will allow you to skip quickly through the slides in a presentation), then click on the 'Slide Show' icon in the bottom left of the screen to start the show from the beginning. When the first slide has finished animating, click once with the left mouse button to move on to the second slide, which should also animate automatically. If you're happy with the way the slide animates, click twice more to return to the editing screen then save your work; otherwise return to the animation settings and change them until you are happy with them.

Creating the third slide

To create the third slide, make sure you are looking at the last slide of the presentation so far (this should be Slide 2) and click *Insert > New Slide* again; a blank slide with a coloured background should appear.

Two pictures need to be added to this slide: **Stairs.gif** and **Footsteps.gif**. See the 'Adding a picture' section above for detailed information on how to add pictures to a slide. For simplicity when ordering the animation of these objects, make sure you add **Stairs.gif** before you add **Footsteps.gif** – this will mean that **Stairs.gif** is 'Picture frame 1' and **Footsteps.gif** is 'Picture frame 2'.

Using the text box tool, add a text box to the slide as described in the 'Adding text' section above. The wording for this slide needs to read:

> Behind the old, old door
> were some old, old steps.

Position the three elements of the page on the slide by 'clicking and dragging' them with the mouse. It's possible that some of the objects will 'disappear' behind one another on this slide. If this happens, select the object that is covering what you want to see by clicking on it with the left mouse button, then select *Draw > Order > Send to back* from the 'Drawing' toolbar, which should put this object behind those that it is covering.

Open up the 'Custom Animation' dialogue box by right-clicking on any of the objects on the slide and selecting 'Custom Animation' from the menu that appears.

Each of the three elements of the slide needs animating this time. Click on 'Object 1' in the 'Timing' section, then click on 'Animate' and set the animation settings for the stairs in the 'Effects' section. (You can make sure that 'Picture frame 1' is the picture of the stairs by looking at the small window in the top right of the screen – eight small boxes

should appear around the image that is 'Picture frame 1', and this should be the stairs.) Set the stairs to 'Dissolve' in the left-hand box, and add **Crack.wav** as a sound effect from the Clip Art folder (the 'Adding sound' section above will show how to do this).

'Picture frame 2' should be the picture of footsteps. Highlight this in the 'Timing' section, click 'Animate' next to it, then set the animation to 'Dissolve' and the sound effect to **Swish.wav** in the 'Effects' section. (Because you have already used **Swish.wav** on the first slide, it will already be listed on the sound effects menu so you don't need to add it again, just select it from the drop-down list.)

Lastly, the text needs animating. Select 'Text 3' and 'Animate' in the 'Timing' section, then set the animation to 'Fly From Top' in the 'Effects' section. No sound needs to accompany this animation, but set the text to appear 'By Word' on the right-hand side.

Check the order in which the objects animate in the window at the top of the dialogue box. Initially, the objects should be set to animate in numerical order, but you want the text to appear in between the

two images. Highlight 'Text 3' and click the 'Move up' button to change the order to 'Picture frame 1', 'Text 3', 'Picture frame 2'. Check also that each item is set to animate 'Automatically' in the 'Timing' section.

Preview the slide to make sure all the animation options are correct, then click 'OK' to return to the main screen. If you wish, run through the whole slide show to see how it is progressing by pressing PAGE UP twice to get to the first slide, then running the slide show as before. You should only need to click the mouse to move between the slides because all the other animations are set to happen automatically. When you are happy, save your work.

Creating the fourth slide

The process for creating the fourth slide is similar to that for the previous slides. Go to the end of the presentation (press PAGE DOWN until you see Slide 3) and click *Insert > New Slide*.

Add two Clip Art images to this slide: **Bats.gif** and **Old chest.gif** (add **Bats.gif** first to keep the animation order simple), and then use the text box tool to add the following text:

> At the top of the old, old steps
> was an old, old chest.

Position the elements on the page by 'clicking and dragging' them with the mouse until you are happy with the layout, then right-click **Bats.gif** and choose 'Custom Animation' to bring up the 'Custom Animation' dialogue box.

Bats.gif should be animated first, and set to 'Spiral', accompanied by **Aliens.wav** as a sound effect. Change the settings for **Old chest.gif** to 'Fly From Bottom Right' accompanied by **Thunder.wav**, and for the text to 'Fly From Top' and to appear 'By Word'.

In the 'Timing' section, make sure that all the items animate 'Automatically', and that they appear in the order: 'Picture frame 1' (**Bats.gif**), 'Text 3', 'Picture frame 2' (**Old chest.gif**). Preview the slide and, if you're happy with the animation, click 'OK' and save your work.

Creating the fifth slide

The steps you have been following for the last three slides should be becoming familiar. You'll be glad to hear they are just the same for the next two!

Insert a new slide at the end of the presentation by clicking *Insert > New Slide*. Add two Clip Art images: **Old chest.gif** and **Hats.gif** (add the images in this order for simplicity) and use the text box tool to add the following text:

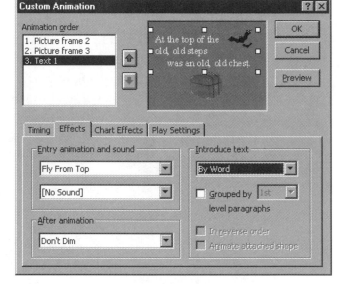

In the old, old chest
were some old, old hats.

'Click and drag' the items around the screen until you are happy with the layout. You may need to change **Hats.gif** so it is in front of **Old chest.gif** (select **Hats.gif** by clicking on it, then click *Draw > Order > Bring to front*).

Right-click on **Old chest.gif** and select 'Custom Animation' to bring up the 'Custom Animation' dialogue box. In the 'Timing' section, make sure that each of the three objects animates automatically. In the 'Effects' section, set **Old chest.gif** ('Picture frame 1') to 'Dissolve', accompanied by **Thunder.wav** as a sound effect. Set **Hats.gif** ('Picture frame 2') to 'Fly From Right', accompanied by **Crack.wav**, and 'Text 3' to 'Fly From Top', with the text appearing 'By Word' (no sound effect is required for the text animation).

The order of the animation for this slide should be 'Picture frame 1', 'Text 3', 'Picture frame 2', and all three should animate automatically. When you are happy with the animation of the slide, click 'OK' and save your work.

To look at the presentation so far, press PAGE UP until you reach Slide 1, then click the Slide Show icon in the bottom left-hand corner of the screen.

Creating the sixth slide

Create a new slide at the end of the presentation as before, and add the Clip Art images **Hats.gif** and **Box.gif** (inserting the images in this order), and the text as below:

Under the old, old hats
was an old, old box.

'Click and drag' the items around the screen with the mouse until you are happy with the layout. You may need to change **Hats.gif** so it is in front of **Box.gif** (select **Hats.gif** by clicking on it, then click *Draw > Order > Bring to front*).

Bring up the 'Custom Animation' dialogue box by right-clicking on **Hats.gif** and selecting 'Custom Animation'. Set the animation properties for 'Picture frame 1' (**Hats.gif**) to 'Fly From Right' (no sound is needed for this animation). 'Object 2' (**Box.gif**) should have an animation setting of 'Dissolve', and be accompanied by **Thunder.wav** from the drop-down list of sound effects that have already been used. The text should be set to 'Fly From Top' and 'By Word'.

In the 'Timing' section, make sure that all three items animate automatically, and that the order of objects is set to 'Picture frame 1', 'Text 3' and 'Picture frame 2'. Preview the animation of the slide if you wish, and when you are happy with the order click 'OK' to return to the main screen. Don't forget to save your work!

Creating the seventh slide

This slide is a little more complex. The animation on this page can be simplified if you wish so the key just flies across the screen and clicks but, for the more adventurous teacher, why not try following the detailed steps below to create a key that twists and turns! This is the most complicated action of the whole presentation – it involves three animations flowing together to create the impression of a turning key, but it is effective! Follow the steps below for an easy guide.

Firstly create a new slide at the end of the presentation as normal. Use the text box tool to add two separate sections of text. At the top of the page, add an object ('Text 1'):

On top of the old, old box
was a key!

And in a separate box ('Text 2') at the bottom, type:

Turn and turn
click and clack

9 : Animated books

It is good if this text can be centred across the slide. To do this, move the pointer to the start of the text in one of the boxes, then click, hold and drag the mouse to the end of the text; the words should be highlighted. Now use the 'Formatting' toolbar to centre the text inside the text box. Do this for both text boxes, and align them across the middle of the slide.

Right-click on the first text box, select 'Custom Animation' and set the animation properties of 'Text 1' to 'Fly From Top' and 'By Word'. Set the properties for 'Text 2' to 'Swivel' and 'All at once', to make this sentence appear as if it is spinning on to the screen. When you are happy with these animations, click 'OK'.

Use the 'Centre' tool (highlighted) to change the alignment of the text.

A turning key

Creating the key the simple way

To create the basic key animation, add the Clip Art image **Key 1.gif** to the slide, and use the mouse to resize and position the image as you wish (see 'Adding a picture' for more information).

Right-click on **Key 1.gif** and choose 'Custom Animation'. When the 'Custom Animation' dialogue box appears, tick the box next to 'Picture frame 3' in the top-left box, and set the animation properties to 'Fly From Left', accompanied by **Lock click.wav** as a sound effect.

In the 'Timing' section, make sure that all three objects on the slide so far animate automatically, and that 'Picture frame 3' comes in between 'Text 1' and 'Text 2'. Preview this to make sure that you are happy with the animation order, then click 'OK'.

If this is sufficient animation of the key for you, then skip the next section and go on to the 'Creating the eighth slide' section. Otherwise, read on!

Creating the key with more complicated animation

The 'twisting key' effect has to be created in three stages, the first of which you will already have done above.

Now, you need to add two more key images on top of the one that's already there. These will appear like a computerised 'flick book', creating the illusion of a turning key.

Insert two more Clip Art images to the slide: **Key 2.gif**, and another copy of **Key 1.gif** (if you add them in this order, it makes the animation easier). Using the mouse, resize them so they are the same size as the first copy of **Key 1.gif** that you added earlier, then position each of the three images on top of one another – **Key 1.gif** at the bottom, **Key 2.gif** in the middle, and the additional copy of **Key 1.gif** on the very top. Don't worry that the images all cover one another up at the moment – when animated, the images will appear in sequence.

Right-click on the top key image and bring up the 'Custom Animation' dialogue box. The first key image ('Picture frame 3') will already be animated and will be listed in the window in the top left-hand corner of the dialogue box, as should 'Text 1' and 'Text 2'.

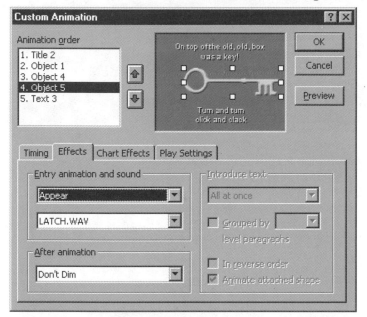

Highlight 'Picture frame 4' (which should be **Key 2.gif**) in the 'Timing' section and click 'Animate'. This image needs to appear on top of the first copy of **Key 1.gif** (it doesn't need to fly in from the side, as the first image has already done this), so set the animation to 'Appear' in the 'Effects' section. Do the same for 'Picture frame 5', which should be the second copy of **Key 1.gif**, and add the sound effect **Latch.wav** to complete the turning of the key.

If you preview the animation thus far, you should see the key fly in from the side of the screen, then the other two images should appear on top of this – but you will have to be quick to see them! The 'Timing' settings need to be changed to put a delay in between each of the key images appearing.

In the 'Timing' section, make sure that you have the objects animating in the correct order: 'Text 1' should be first, followed by 'Picture frame 3', 'Picture frame 4' and 'Picture frame 5' (the three key images in succession) and lastly 'Text 2'. Highlight any that are not in the correct order, and use the 'Move Up' and 'Move Down' buttons to change the order.

Each item on the screen should be set to animate automatically, but 'Picture frame 4' and 'Picture frame 5' need a pause adding. To do this, highlight each item individually in the top left-hand box and change the 'Start animation' setting to 'Automatically' in the 'Timing' section. Then point to the box underneath that says '0' and click with the left mouse button inside. This box sets the number of seconds that the computer will wait before carrying out the animation. Set this to two seconds for both 'Picture frame 4' and 'Picture frame 5'. Preview the animation, and you should see the key animation happen a lot more slowly. Click 'OK' when you are happy with the settings.

To see this slide properly, click the 'Slide Show' icon in the bottom left-hand corner of the screen. Hopefully the key will animate correctly, and you will hear the lock click as the key turns. Don't forget to save your work!

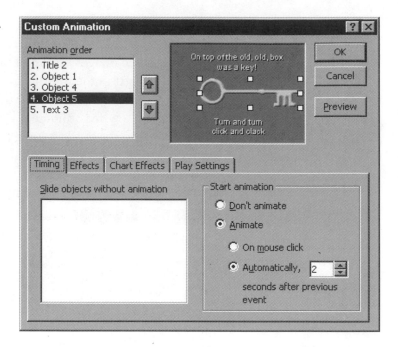

Creating the eighth slide

This is a simple slide to create as it only contains text! Insert a new slide at the end of the presentation, then use the text box tool to create two text boxes. In the first text box ('Text 1'), add:

In the old, old, box

And in the second ('Text 2'), add:

Was...
　　was...
　　　　a...

Use the TAB key to move the text across the page. To add more impact, make the text in the second box larger and bolder (you could change the colour of individual words as well).

Right-click on the first text box and select 'Custom Animation' to bring up the 'Custom Animation' dialogue box. Both text boxes need to be animated, so select both in the 'Timing' section. In the 'Effects' section, 'Text 1' should be set to 'Fly From Top' and 'By Word'; 'Text 2' should be set to 'Fly From Left' and 'By Word', and should be accompanied by **Thunder.wav** from the drop-down list of sound effects.

Make sure both items are set to animate automatically in the 'Timing' section, then preview your work, click 'OK' and save the file.

134

Draw ▾ | ⬚ | AutoShapes ▾ | ╲ ⬉ □ ○ 📰 ◀ | 🖊 ▾ 🖌 ▾ A ▾ | ≡ ≣ ⇄ ▣ ◱

| Slide 8 of 10 | Blank Presentation |

🏁 Start | 🖥 Microsoft PowerPoint... | 📷 Adobe Photoshop | 🎵 [00] 00:00 - CD Player | 📸 SnagIt Capture Preview

Creating the ninth slide

To create the 'GHOST' writing for this page, WordArt has been used. This is a useful option that can be used to create words in interesting shapes in most *Microsoft* applications. Click the 'Insert WordArt' icon on the bottom toolbar. From the menu that appears, select the shape you want the word to be (in the example on the CD, 'Cascade up' – bottom row, fourth from left – has been used, but you can choose any style you like) then click 'OK'. An 'Edit WordArt' text box will appear.

Delete the 'Your Text Here' message and replace it with 'GHOST!', and change the font and size if you wish (Arial Black and 36pt are good settings, although you can change these later). Click 'OK' to create your WordArt.

WordArt Gallery

Select a WordArt style:

Choose a design for your WordArt from the selection on offer.

If the text appears too small, or in the wrong position, use the mouse to select the text, then 'click and drag' the corners of the WordArt until it is the right size and in the right position.

You must also add the ghost to this slide – insert the Clip Art file **Ghost.gif** from the 'Workshop components' folder and 'click and drag' to resize and position the picture until you are happy with the layout.

To animate the slide, right-click on the WordArt and select 'Custom Animation'. In the dialogue box that appears, tick both 'WordArt: cascade up 1' and 'Picture frame 2'. Set the animation properties for 'WordArt: cascade up 1' to 'Fly From Bottom-left', and for 'Picture frame 2' to 'Fly From Right', accompanied by **Evil laugh.wav** as a sound effect. Make sure that both will appear automatically in the 'Timing' section, and when you are happy with the order of the animation, click 'OK' and save your work.

Creating the tenth slide

To create the final slide, insert a new slide at the end of the presentation. Using the text box tool, create a text box and type 'The End!' into the box. Style the text as you wish (this text could be larger

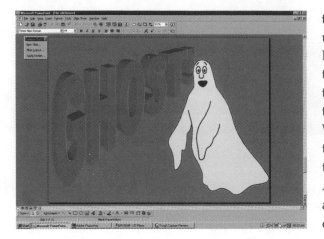

than normal text you have used before). Insert a copy of **Bats.gif** as Clip Art to finish the presentation off, using the mouse to 'click and drag' the items into position. When you are happy with the layout, right-click on the text box, choose 'Custom Animation' and set the animation properties in the dialogue box that appears.

The settings for 'Text 1' should be 'Fly From Top' and 'By Word'. 'Picture frame 2' should be set to 'Spiral' and should be accompanied by **Aliens.wav**. Check that both objects animate automatically in the 'Timing' section, then click 'OK' and save your work.

This completes your animated storybook! To see how the whole slide show looks from start to finish, press PAGE UP until you reach the first slide of the presentation, then click the 'Slide Show' icon in the bottom left-hand corner of the screen to start the show. You should only have to click the left mouse button between each slide – everything else should happen automatically. Remember to click only once between each slide, otherwise you will skip two slides by mistake – this can be a problem on slower computers as there may be a pause between slides and it can be tempting to click again just to make sure. Try to resist the temptation! If you do advance too far by mistake, press 'P' on the keyboard to go back to the previous slide.

If you encounter any problems during the show, hit ESCAPE at any point to quit the show and return to the editing screen on the slide you were last looking at – this will allow you to go back and correct any mistakes.

When you can get from the start of the slide show to the end without any mistakes, save the file. It's now ready to use!

Troubleshooting

If you've followed the instructions above, there shouldn't be any problems when you run the slide show. It is possible, though, that some unexpected things may happen when running through the show. Below are two of the main problems encountered when animating a story.

❑ If pictures and text are animating in the wrong order on a page, double-check the 'Timing' section in the 'Custom Animation' dialogue box. Right-click any object on the slide and select 'Custom Animation' to bring up the dialogue box,

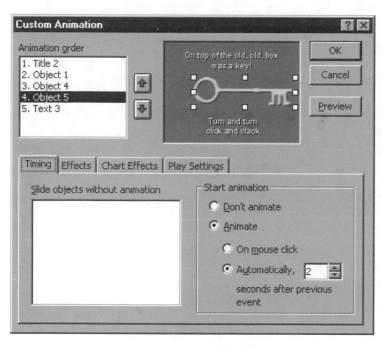

The 'Animation order' section allows you to change the order in which objects animate with the up and down arrows.

then select the 'Timing' section. Highlight each object individually (you will be able to see which object you are working on in the small window in the top right-hand corner of the dialogue box) and use the 'Move Up' and 'Move Down' arrows to change the order. 'Preview' will allow you to check whether the objects are set to animate in the right order.

o   If there is an unexpected pause in the slide show, and pictures or text won't appear until you click the left mouse button, check that all the items on the slide are set to animate automatically in the 'Timing' section of the 'Custom Animation' box.

Conclusion

The principles and examples described here show how to create 'The old house' as a *PowerPoint* presentation, but these techniques can be applied to any story you wish – all you need is appropriate Clip Art and sounds, and the imagination to make the stories come to life!

Animated stories can really capture the children's imaginations, and using repeating patterns and sounds can help them to become familiar with the story very quickly. These animated story books are multimedia in its truest sense.

Adapting the idea

❏ Also included on the CD as a further example of what can be achieved is an animated story called **Hickory dickory dock.ppt**. The Clip Art and sound effects are also included in the 'Workshop components' folder, so you can try making this presentation yourself as well. Feel free to use the finished presentation and components as you wish.

❏   Try creating animation for your own stories, rhymes or poems, such as *Handa's Surprise*, or 'Incy Wincy Spider'. Why not try animating one of the children's own stories? By changing the Clip Art and animation settings you can turn almost any story into an animated book.

❏   Photographs of the children could be animated to create a class movie, or try creating a guided tour of the school. By using a digital camera, photographs, children's

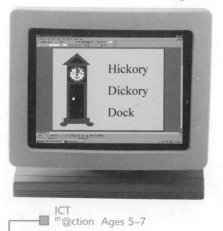

9: Animated books

drawings or paintings can be used in animations quickly and easily –
as long as you can find them on your computer, they can be included
in a *PowerPoint* presentation.

❏ To reinforce literacy work, the colour of certain words in a story
could be changed: nouns highlighted in blue, adjectives highlighted in
red and so on. Try changing the colour of key words or punctuation in
the book.

❏ Children can read animated books for themselves. When they
watch the animated story, all they need to know is that they must click
the left mouse button to 'turn the page'. (If children go too far by
mistake, tell them to press 'P' on the keyboard to go back a step.)

Glossary

@

Part of an e-mail address that separates the individual user's name from the name of their Internet Service Provider. What comes before the '@' tells you who the e-mail is being sent to; what follows tells you where the e-mail is being sent (the 'Service Provider').

Animation

A movement of an individual piece of text or a picture on the computer screen. These can be changed in *PowerPoint* to create a variety of effects.

Application

A program that performs a specific task, such as a word processor or a spreadsheet.

BACKSPACE (often marked ←)

Used to delete a mistake made when typing, BACKSPACE will remove the character immediately to the left of the cursor. The DELETE key will remove the character to the right of the cursor.

Brush (or paintbrush)

A tool used in painting and drawing packages to make marks on screen similar to a real paintbrush, but with less precision than the pencil tool.

CAPS LOCK

Sets the letter keys to type in capital letters without the need to hold down SHIFT for each letter. This should only to be used when writing a whole sentence in capital letters, as using it for individual letters is considered bad practice.

CD-ROM

A circular plastic disc used to store information in a format that can be read by a computer with a CD-ROM drive.

Classify

Putting data into sets based on its properties.

'Click and drag'

Technique used to select and move an object by clicking once on the object with the left mouse button to select it, then holding the left button down and moving the mouse so the on-screen object follows. When the left mouse button is released, the object is placed in its new position.

Computer simulation

Using the computer to create and explore imaginary worlds.

Control

To tell an object or person what to do.

Delete

Erasing text or an object from the computer, much like using an eraser to remove pencil lines on a piece of paper.

Glossary

DELETE key
Used to remove a mistake, text or picture in many applications. The DELETE key can also be used to remove the character to the right of the cursor in a word processor.

Desktop
The main 'work area' of the computer – this is the screen that you see when *Windows* has started up. Files, folders and icons can be kept on the desktop.

Double click
Two clicks in quick succession of the left mouse button, usually to launch an application or open a file directly.

e-mail
Common name for electronic mail: the sending of a message from computer to computer via telephone lines.

ENTER/RETURN
The largest key on the keyboard – used to create a new line in a word processor, to complete data entry in a spreadsheet or to confirm an action.

File
A single document stored on the computer that can be opened by an application. Everything stored on a computer is stored in a file. All files need their own unique name, and can be organised into folders for easy location.

Flood fill
Used in painting and drawing packages to fill enclosed areas of the screen with a selected colour.

Floppy disk
Small plastic disks used to store relatively small amounts of information. Data is atored in a magnetic format that can be read by a computer with a floppy disk drive.

Folder
Similar to a real-life folder – a collection of (normally related) documents or files grouped together in one place so they can easily be located and organised.

Graphics
Term covering different images displayed on the computer. These can be drawings, photos, lines, charts, animations or video.

Hotlinks or **hyperlinks**
Part of a Web page, document or presentation that, when clicked, will take you to another destination either in the same document or to another document.

Icon
A small graphical representation of a function, file or program that can be clicked on and manipulated. When selected they can be moved, deleted, activated or used to perform a function.

Imaginary/faux
Something that is not real.

Information
A group of words, a picture or a sound that tells us something.

Instruction
A statement or series of statements that gives an object a specific command or commands to do something in order to achieve a result.

Key words
The most important pieces of information in a document. These can be used to sort and search through data in order to find relevant and useful information.

Keyboard
The main input device of a computer – pressing any of the letters on the keyboard will usually result in the letter appearing on the screen.

Label
A key word or phrase to describe an object or point out important pieces of information.

Left mouse button
The most commonly used button on the mouse, which is generally pressed once (a 'single click') to select or use a tool, or pressed twice (a 'double click') to confirm an action.

Line tool
Used in painting and drawing packages to draw straight and diagonal lines of different thickness and colours.

Model
A real or fantasy environment created within the computer where different parameters can be tested and changed in order to try and answer a hypothesis, and where the results can be seen instantly on the screen.

Mouse
Pointing device held in the hand and used to control the on-screen pointer by moving the mouse on the desk – the pointer will mimic this movement.

Multimedia
Using more than one way of communicating information (for example, text, sound and video) in the same document. This information is often linked together or integrated so that all the pieces of information relatesto one another.

Glossary

Order
To put a series of instructions one after another so that they can be followed step-by-step to produce a result; also to sort data or information in a database or spreadsheet so that it can be analysed more easily, for example in to alphabetical order.

Pencil tool
Used in graphics and drawing packages to draw freehand lines and shapes of different colours on the page, much the same as a real pencil.

Pictogram
A graph presenting data through columns of pictures.

Pointer (sometimes called a cursor)
Controlled by the movement of the mouse and used to move quickly around the screen, selecting and moving items.

Presentation (sometimes called a slide show)
A collection of animated 'pages' combining text, images and sound together on the computer screen that the user can work through.

Print
Making a paper copy of a document on the computer screen so that work can be taken away and looked at elsewhere, or filed away for reference.

Real-life environment
An environment that really exists, is alive and requires caring for, as opposed to a computer-generated environment that exists only within the computer.

RETURN/ENTER
The largest key on the keyboard – used to create a new line in a word processor, to complete data entry in a spreadsheet or to confirm an action.

Right click
One click of the right mouse button which, when performed on an icon or specific object, often brings up a menu of options or properties relating to the object.

Save as
An option to save a file with a different file name or format from the original file, so that the original is preserved and a new copy is made. This is useful for children when making progressive revisions to their work, and when they may need to keep several copies of their work.

Select
When an object is selected (often by highlighting it or clicking on it with the left mouse button), any menu actions or functions will be performed on only the selected object and will leave the rest of the files, document or page untouched.

Sequence
A set of instructions that have been put in an order to produce a desired effect.

SHIFT key
A key on the keyboard (often marked ⇧), which is used to create a single capital letter; hold the SHIFT key down and press any letter key at the same time to create a capital letter. This is the preferred way to create single capital letters, as opposed to using the CAPS LOCK key.

Shortcut
A quick link to a file or folder on the computer that may otherwise be difficult or long-winded to find. Shortcuts to commonly-used programs, files or folders are often placed on the desktop for easy access.

Simulated environment
Not a real environment but one held entirely inside the computer that doesn't require care in the same way as a real environment.

Single click
One quick click of the left (or right) mouse button, usually to select an object or confirm an action.

Slide
A single 'page' of a multimedia presentation in *Microsoft PowerPoint*.
Sort: arranging a set of data into a useful order so that it can be interpreted more easily.

SPACE bar
The longest key on the keyboard, which is used to create a blank space between words when word processing.

Spray tool
Used in painting and drawing packages to create an effect similar to spray paint on the screen.

Taskbar
The grey bar that is almost always visible and runs along the bottom of the desktop with the 'Start' button on the left – any program that is running is represented by a button on the taskbar, and you can switch between these programs by selecting them on the taskbar. There may also be shortcuts to other commonly used functions or programs that are always on the taskbar, such as the clock, volume control or access to the Internet.

Text
Written language.

Texture
Creating a paint effect on the screen using different combinations of a painting or drawing program's tools.

Glossary

Toolbar
A collection of tools (represented by icons) that are available for use in a program. These often appear in a row along the top or bottom of the screen, and can be customised to incorporate the most commonly used functions.

Tools
The name of individual functions that can be used to create items on the screen, such as a pencil tool to draw lines.

Turn off
To deactivate a device.

Turn on
To activate a device.

Virtual garden
A faux garden that has been created inside the computer; one that is not living and does not need to be cared for in the same way as a real garden.

Word bank
A group of words related to a topic or theme that can be used to support children's work, allowing them to copy the words from the word bank into their own work.